Find exclusive merchandise at
https://damian-draco.printify.me

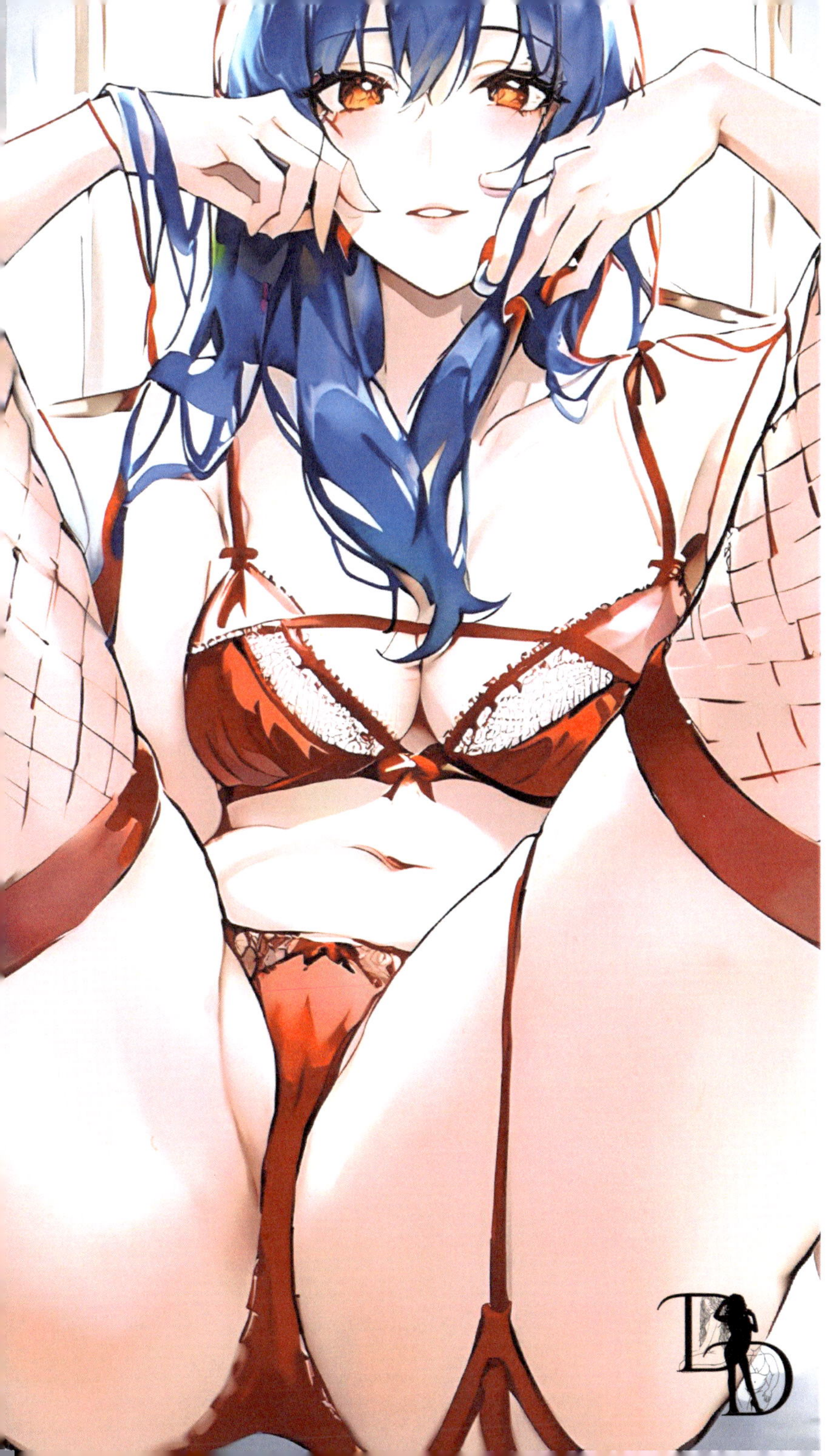

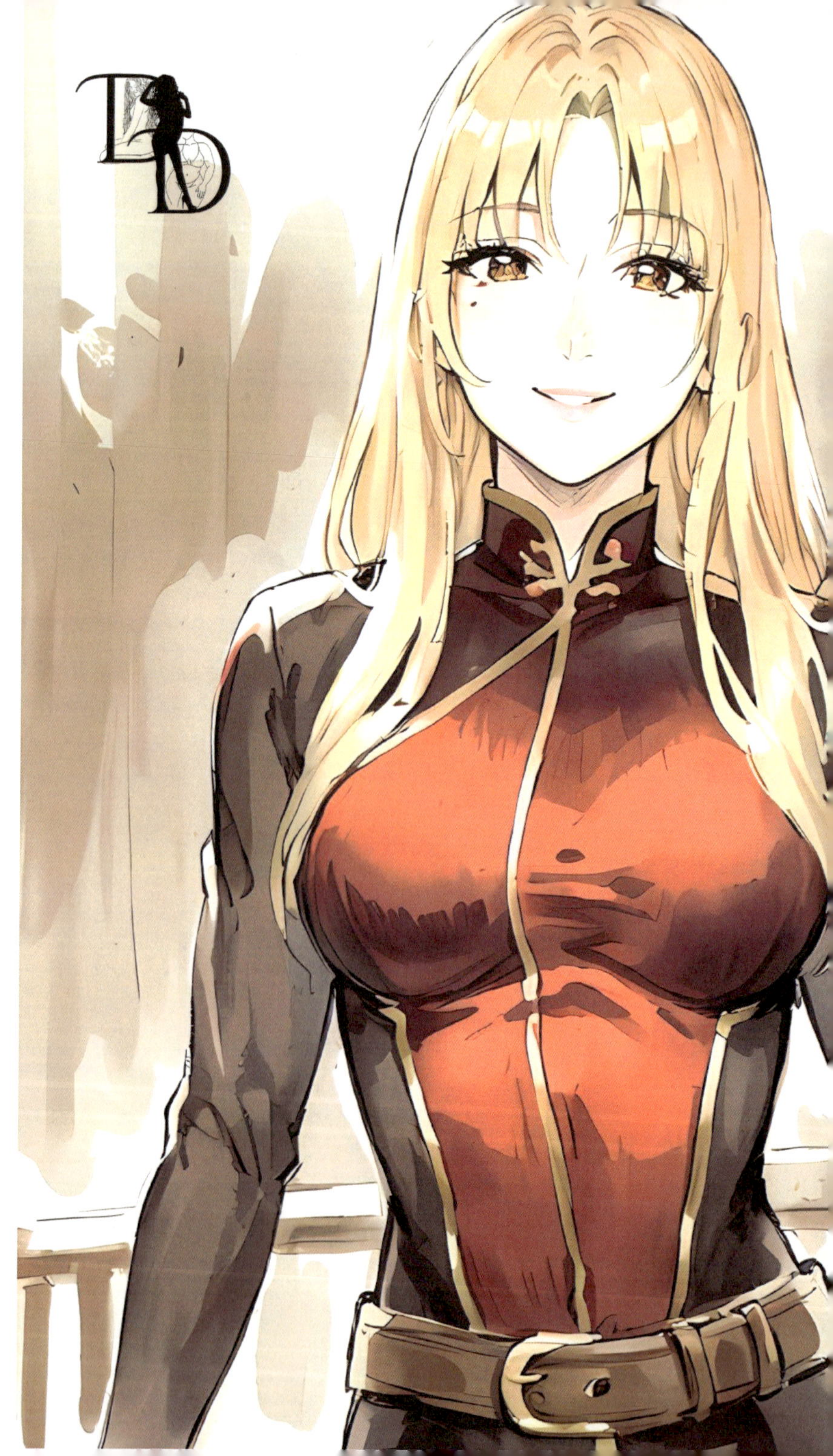

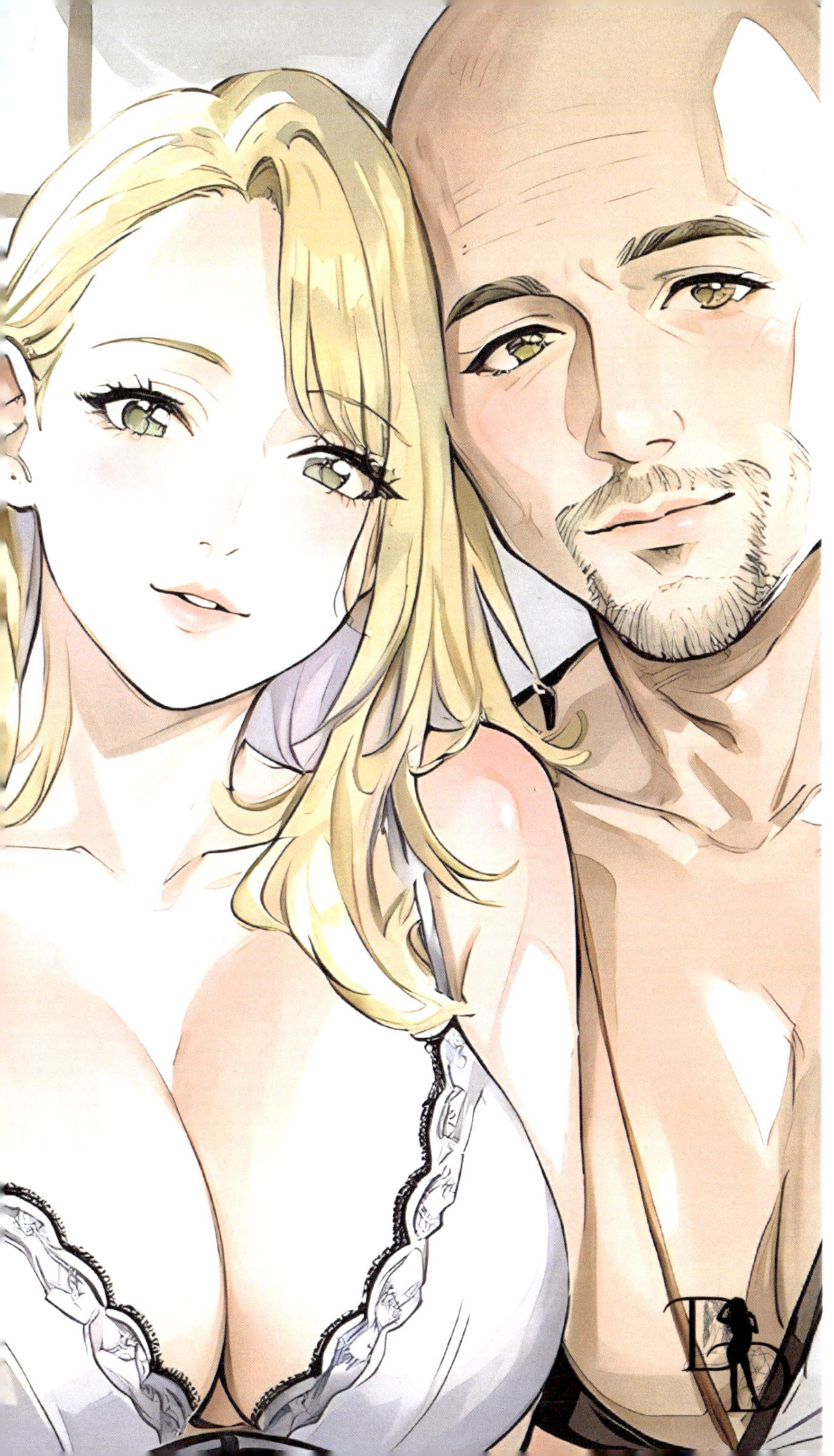

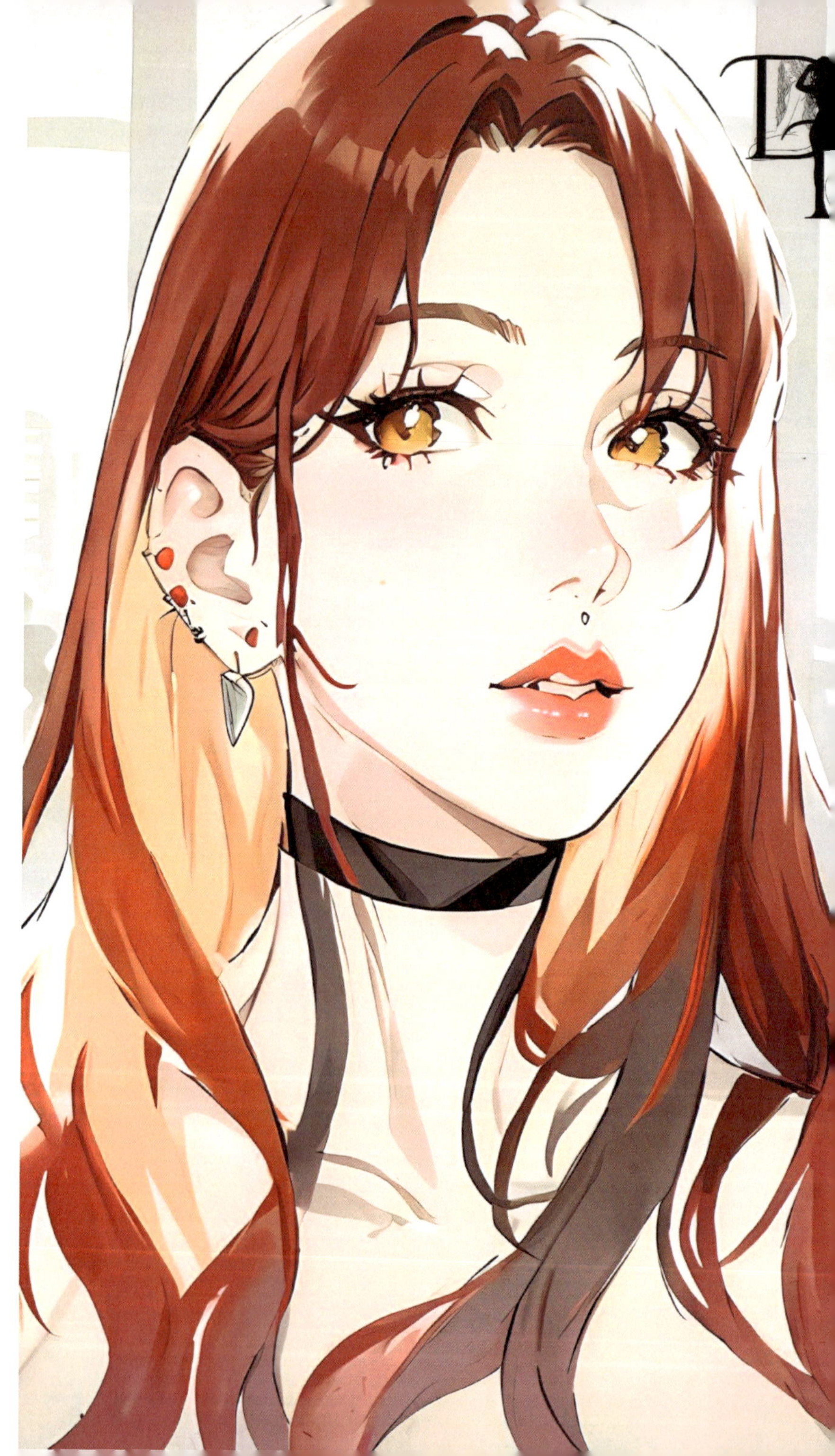

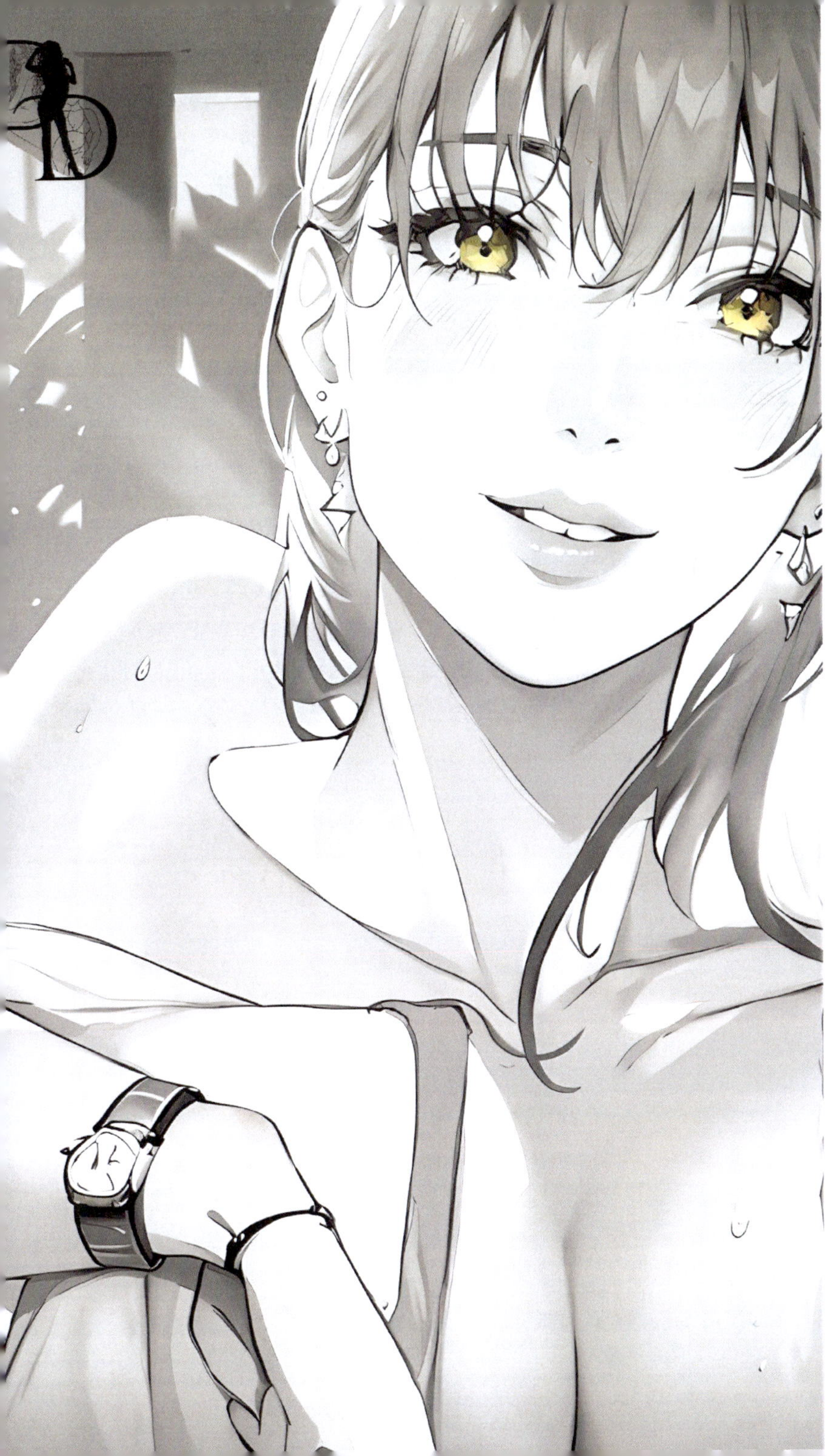

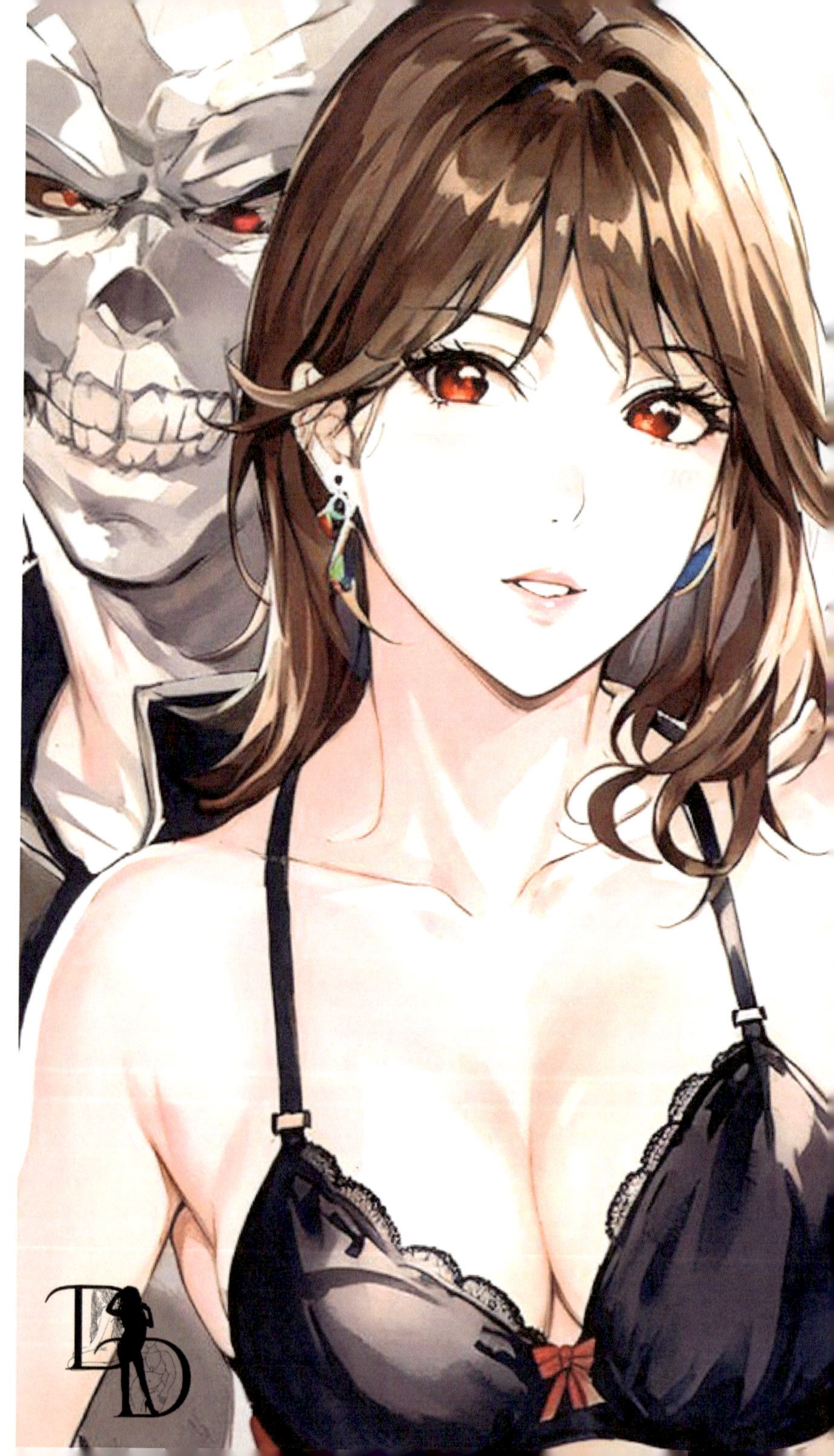

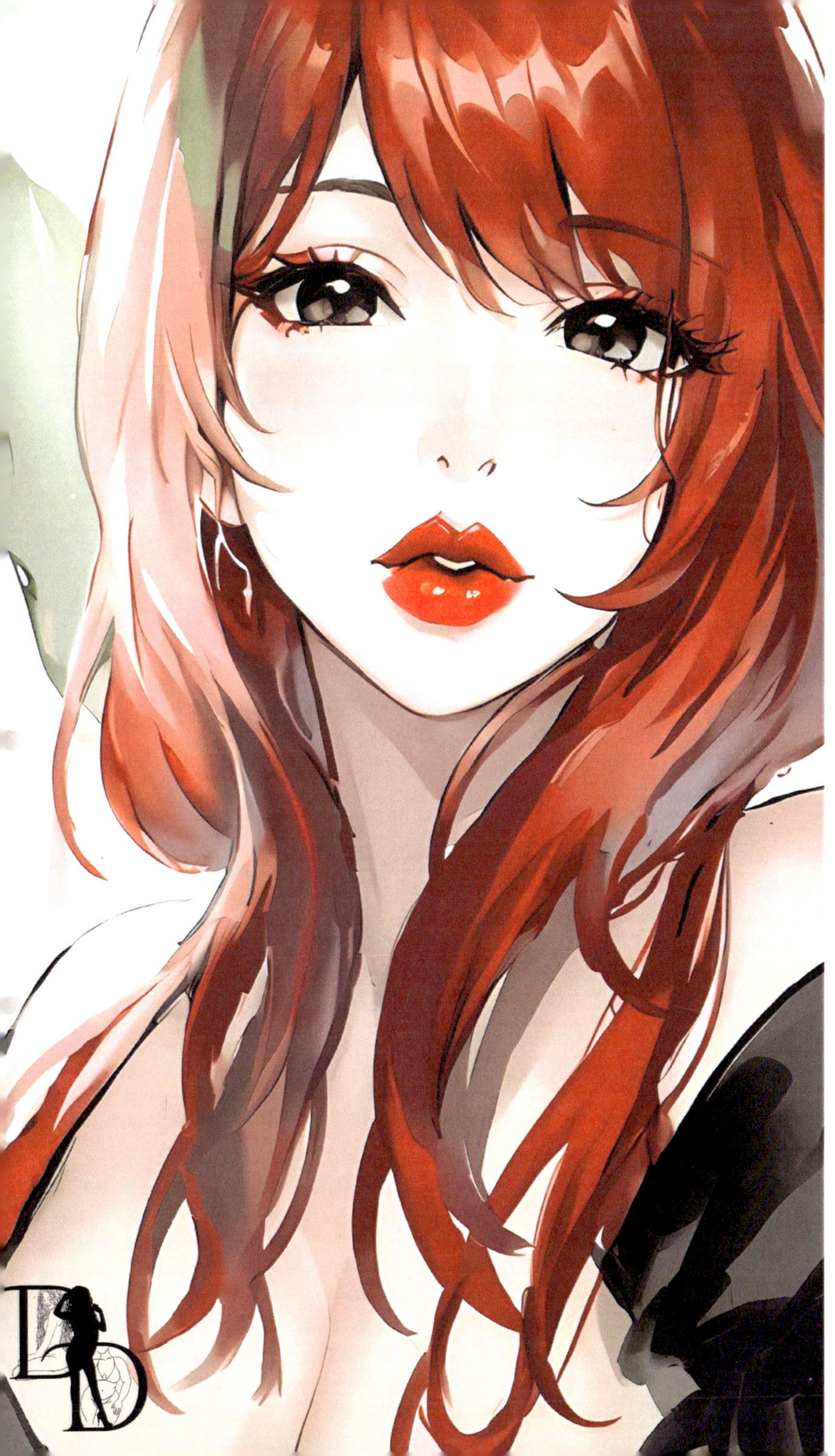

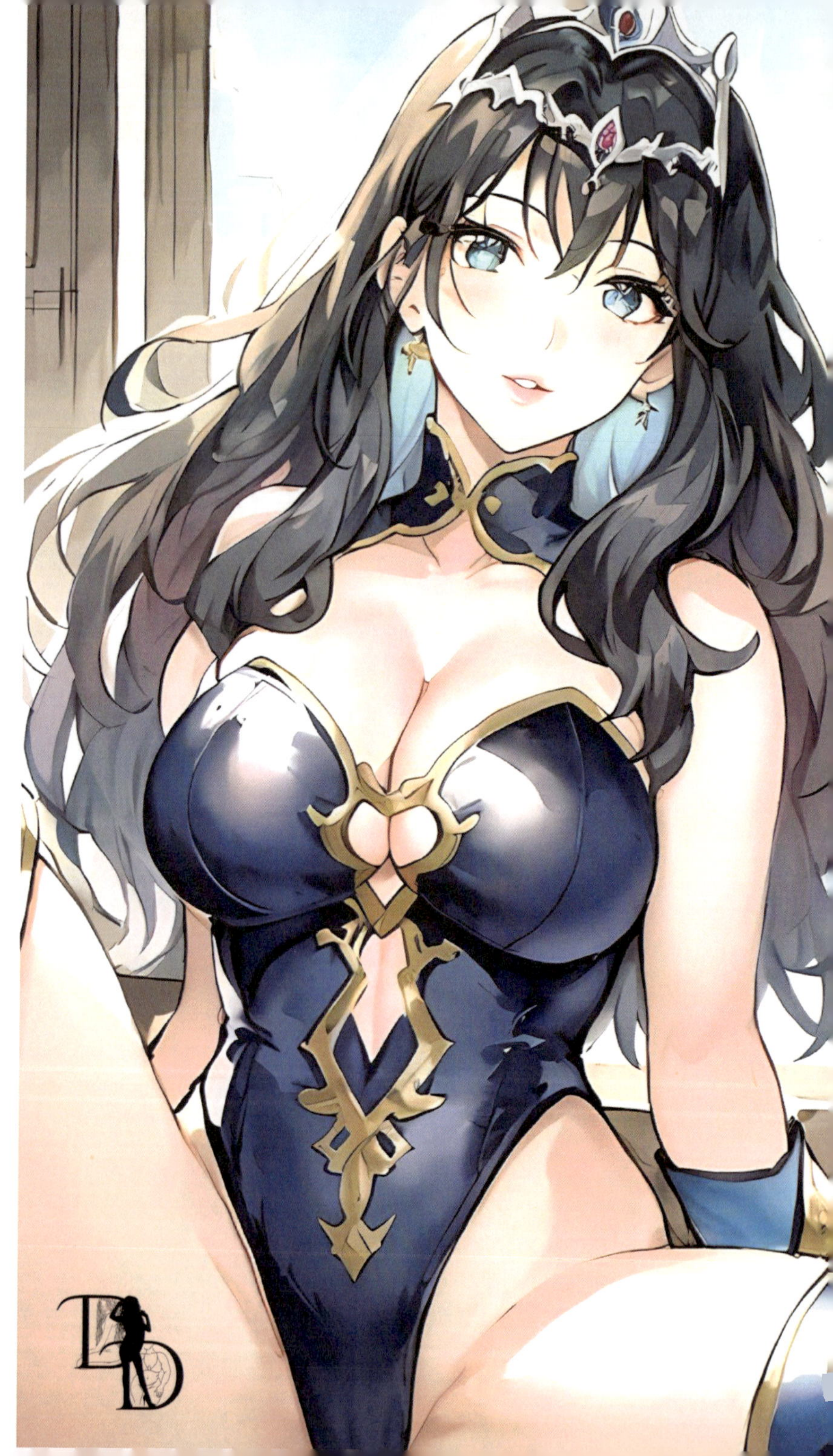

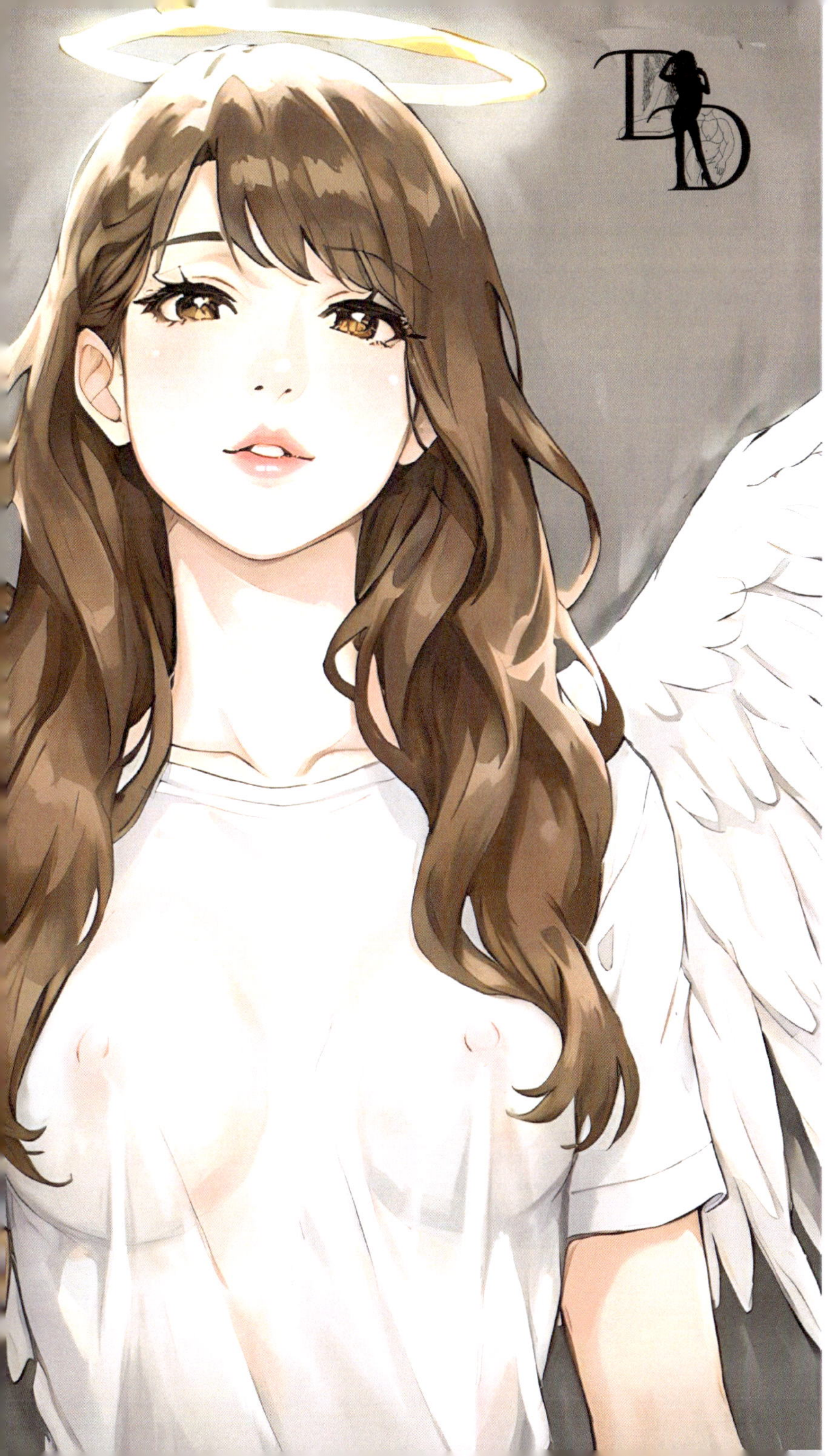

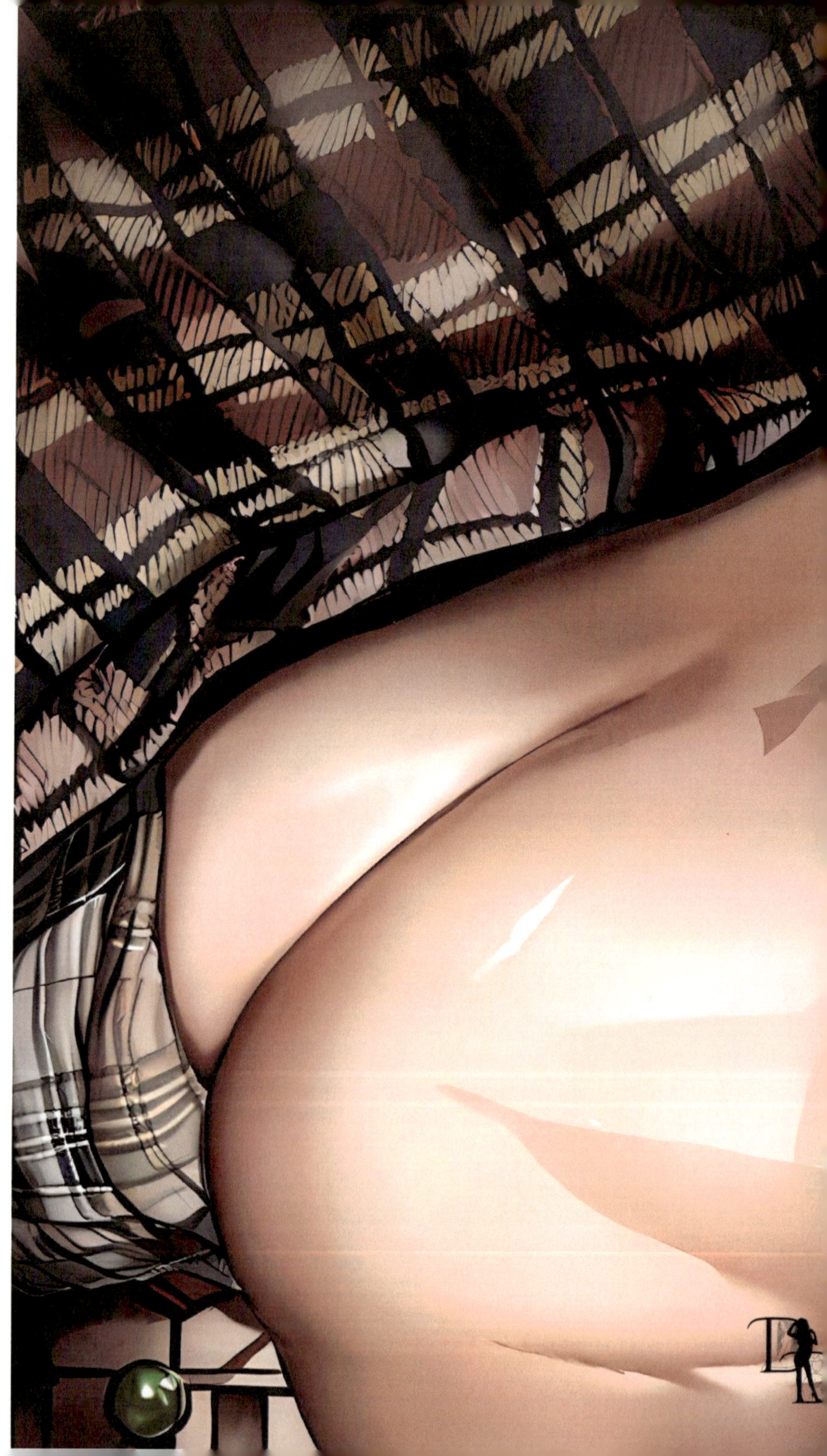

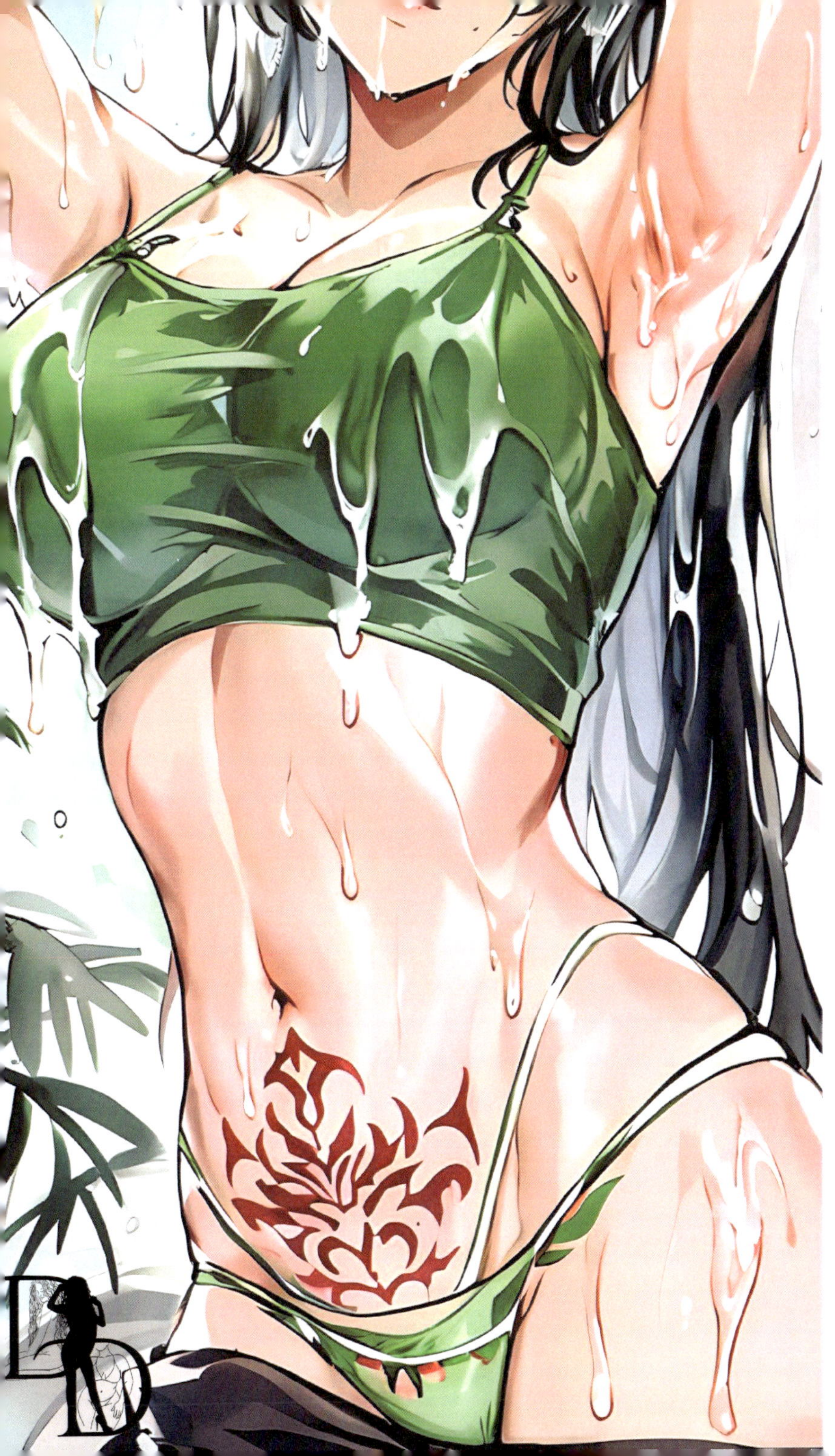

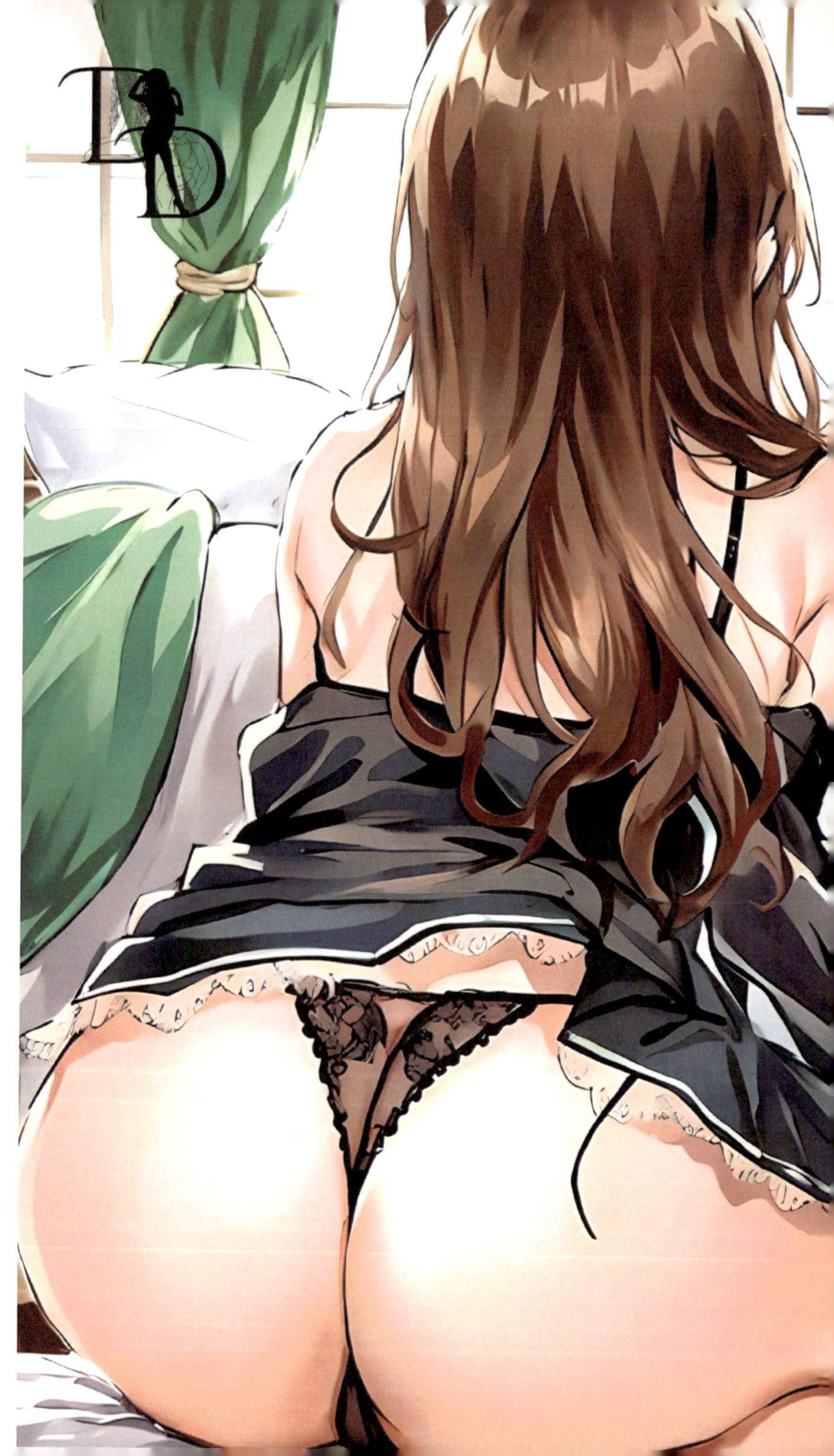

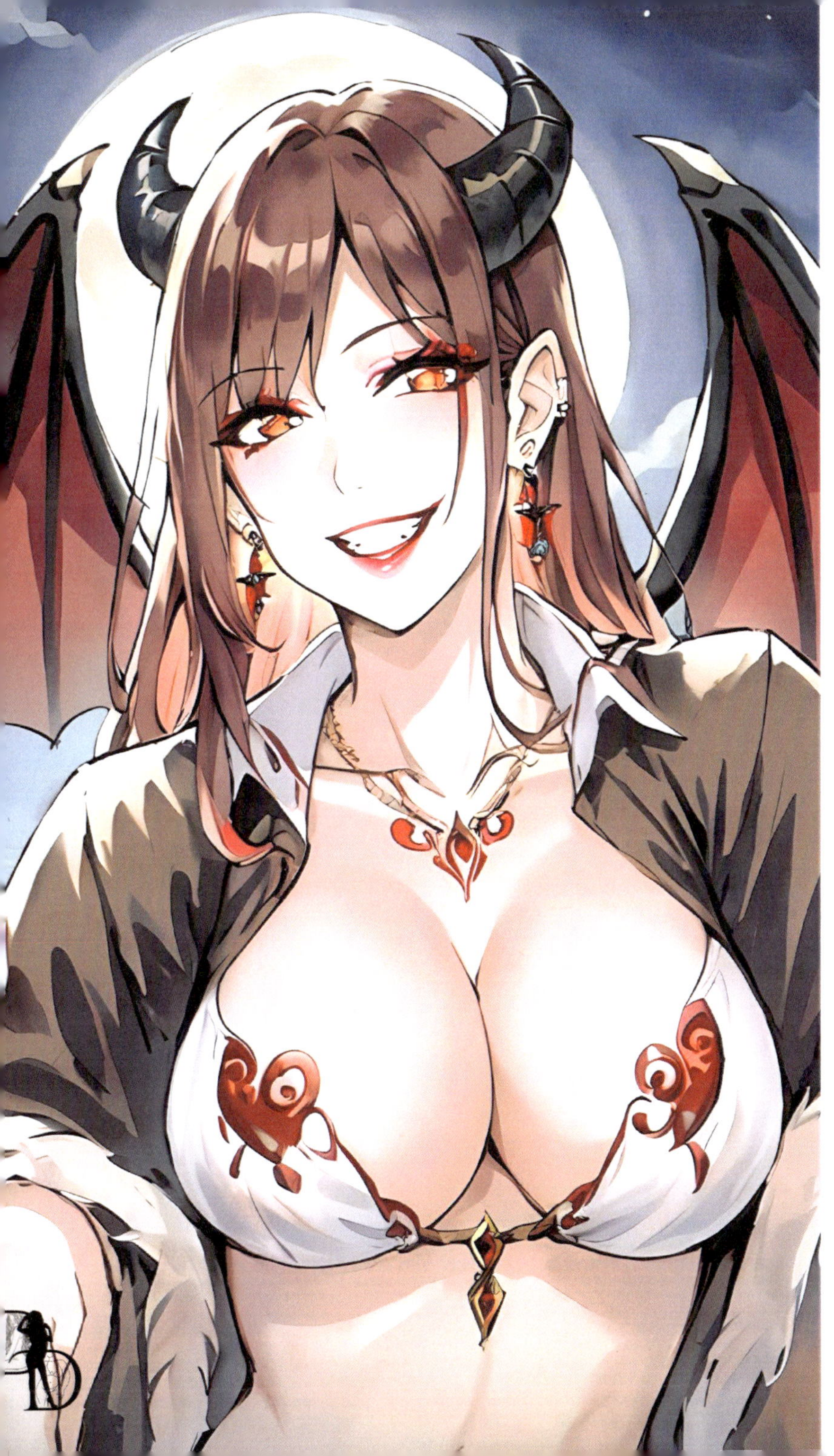

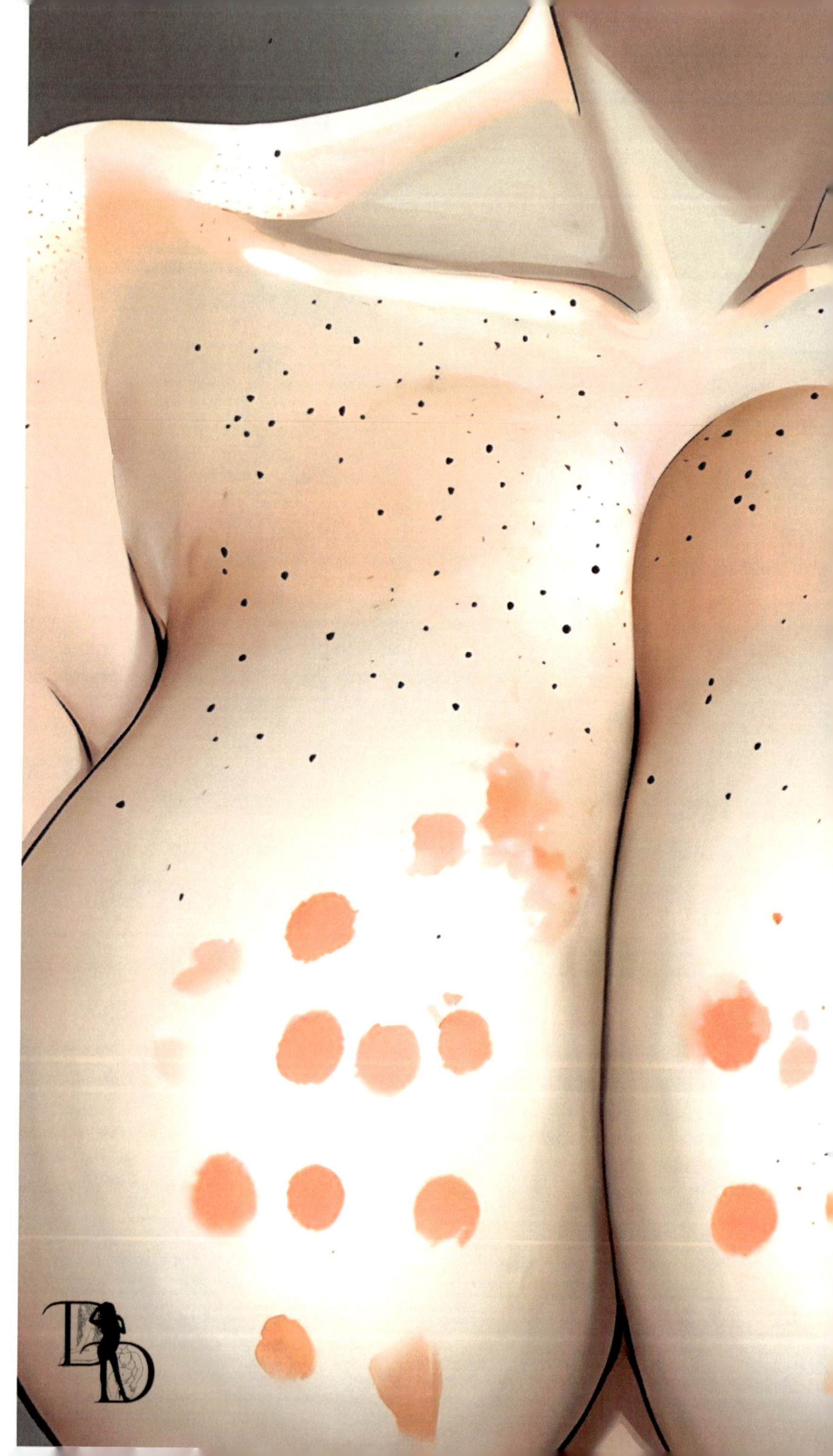

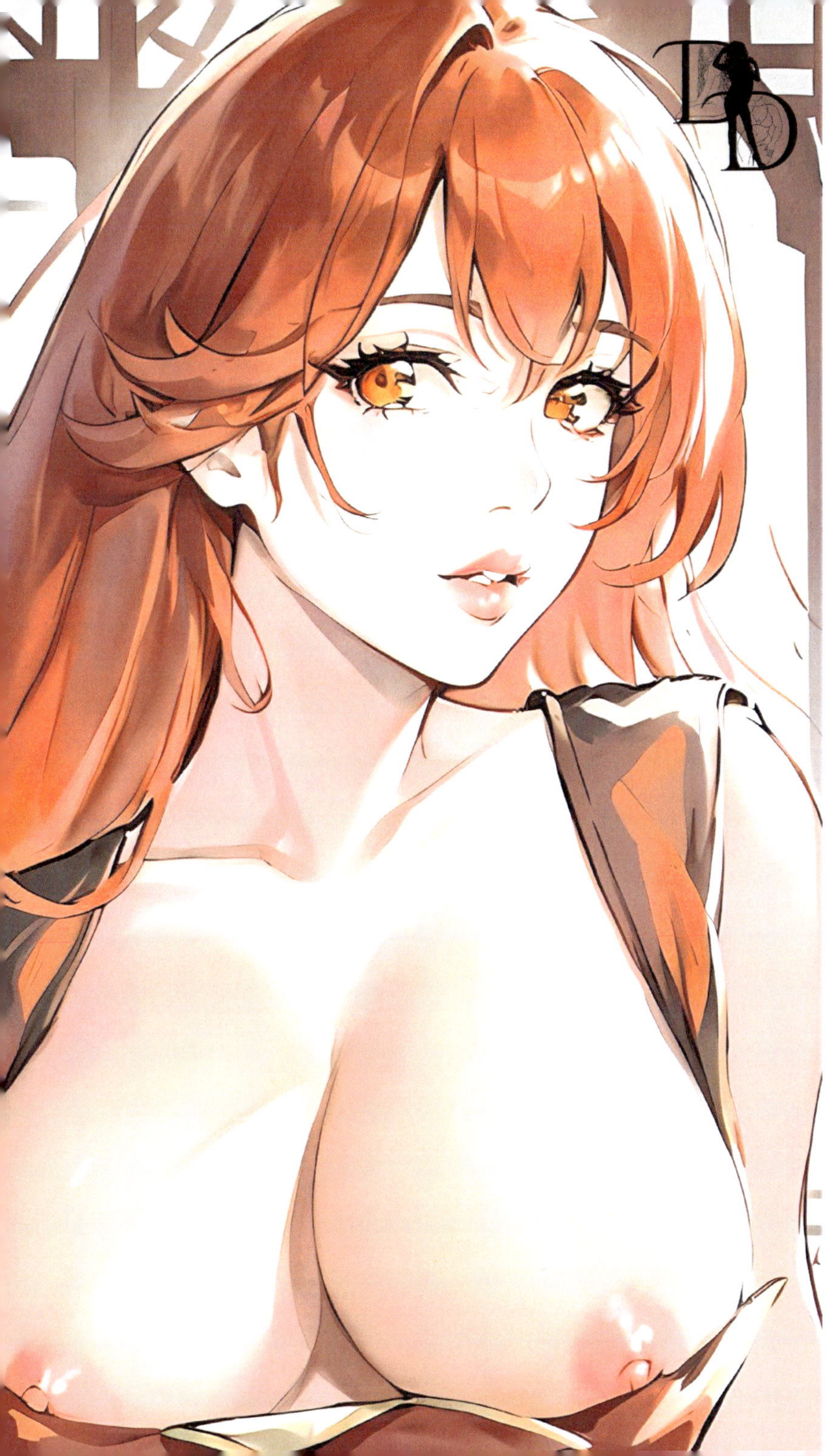

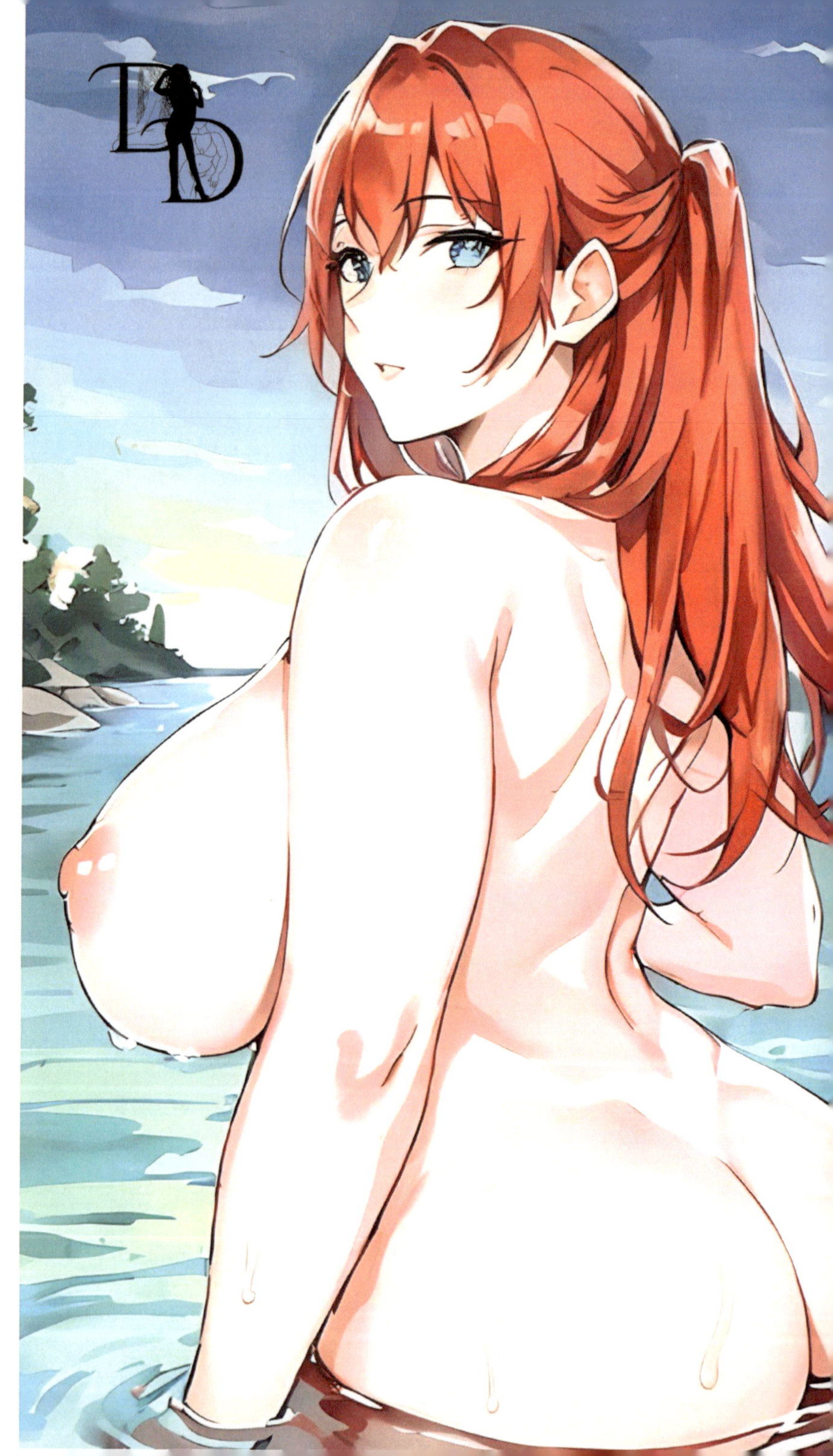

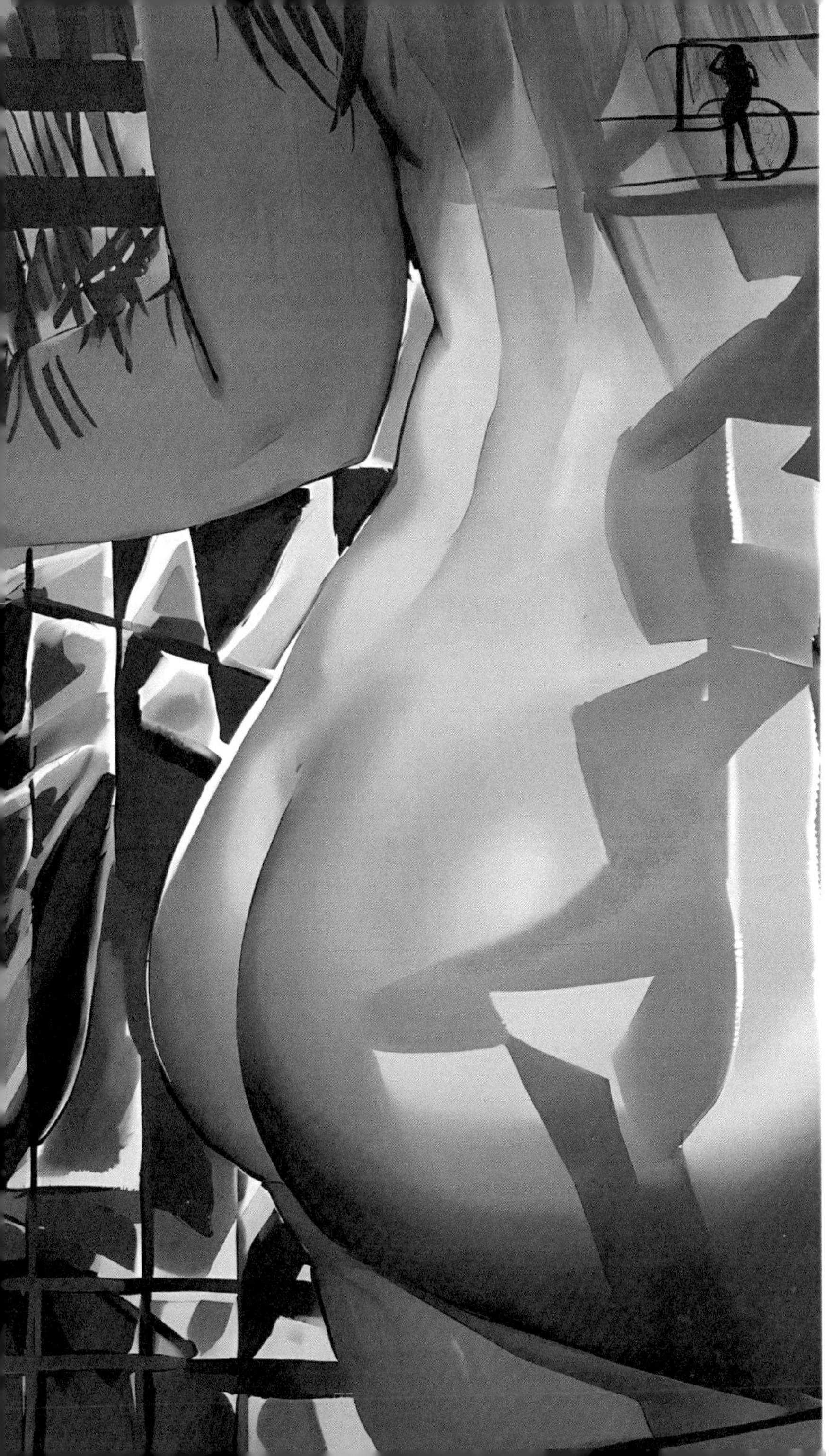

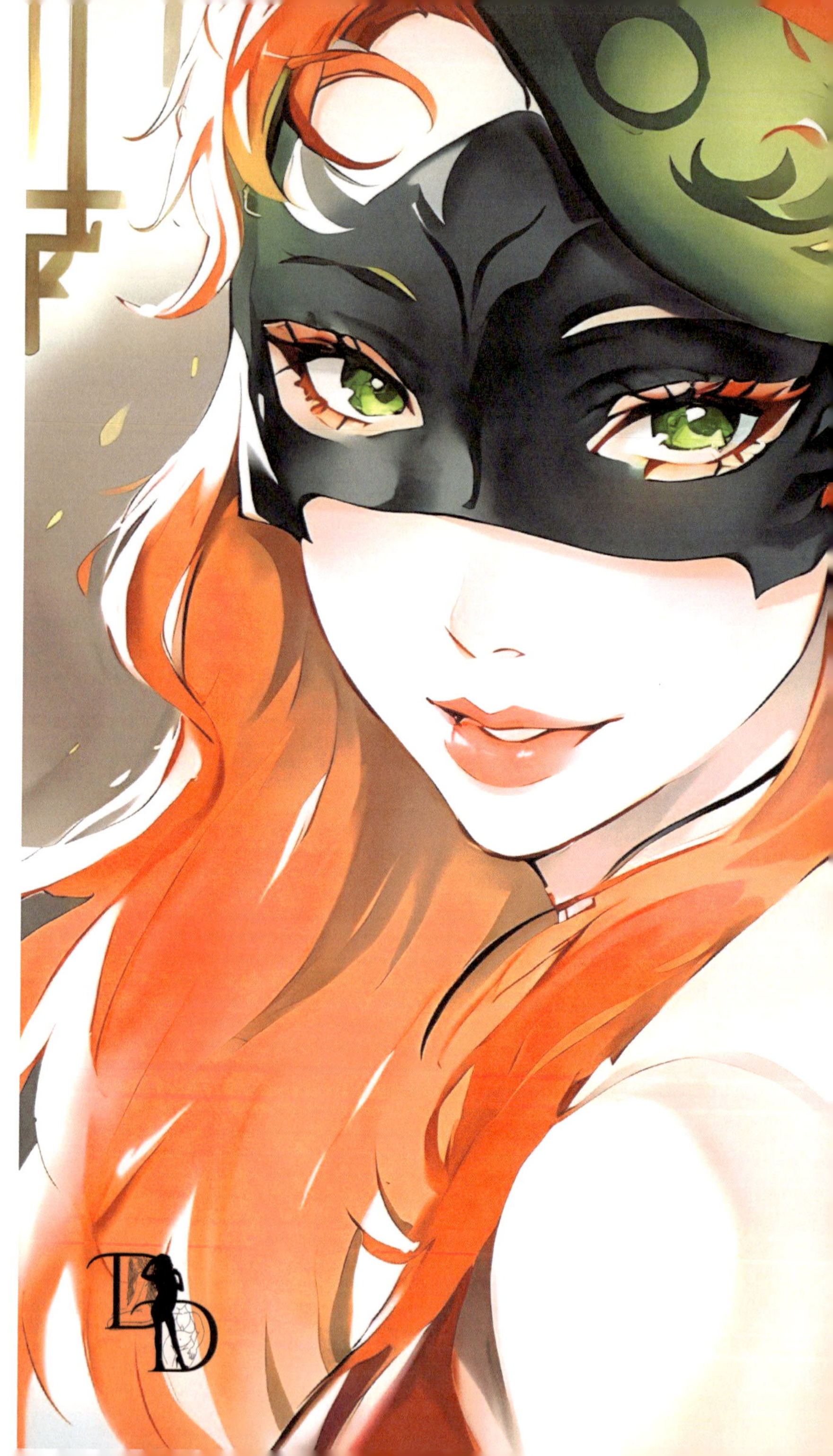

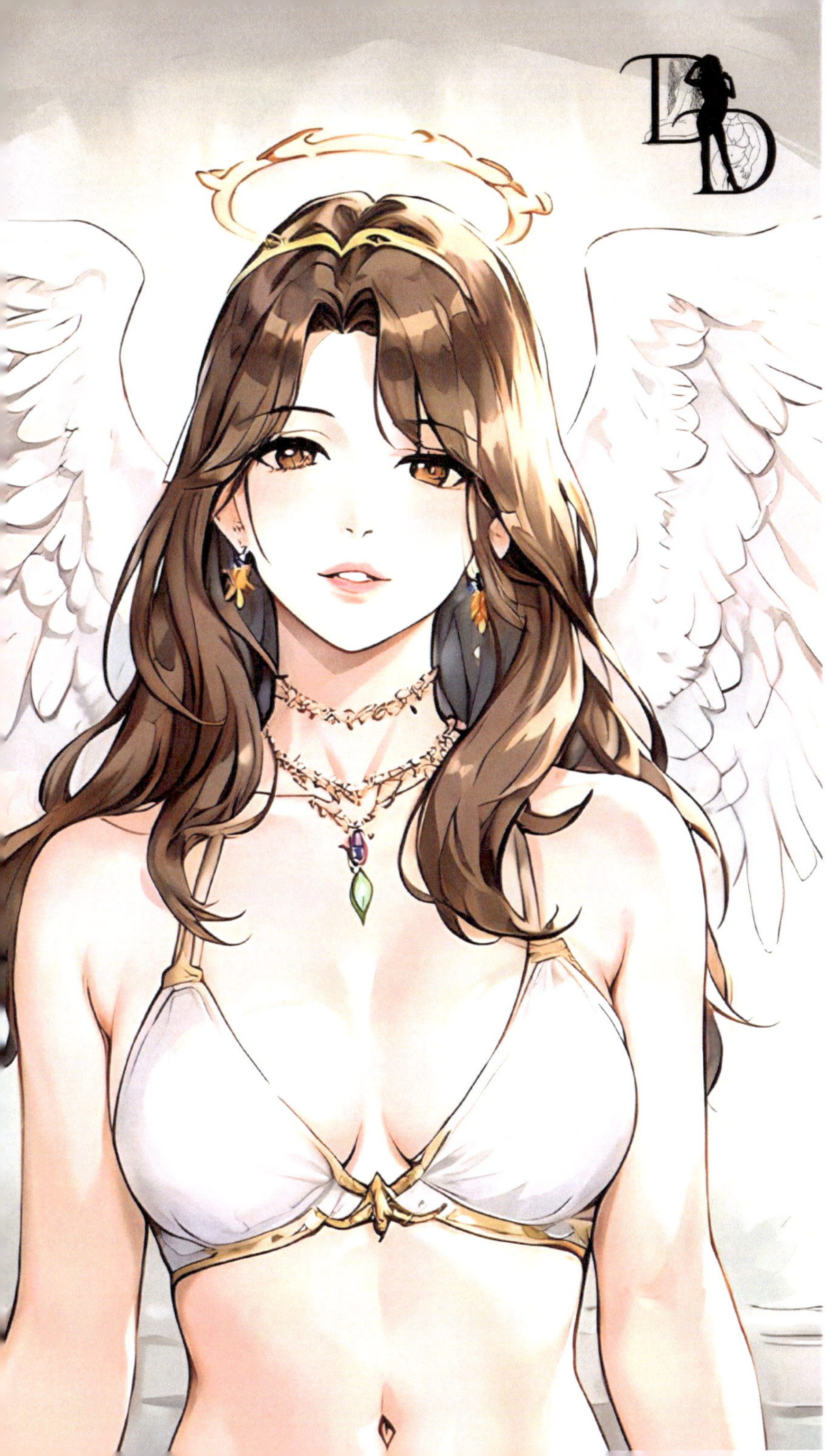

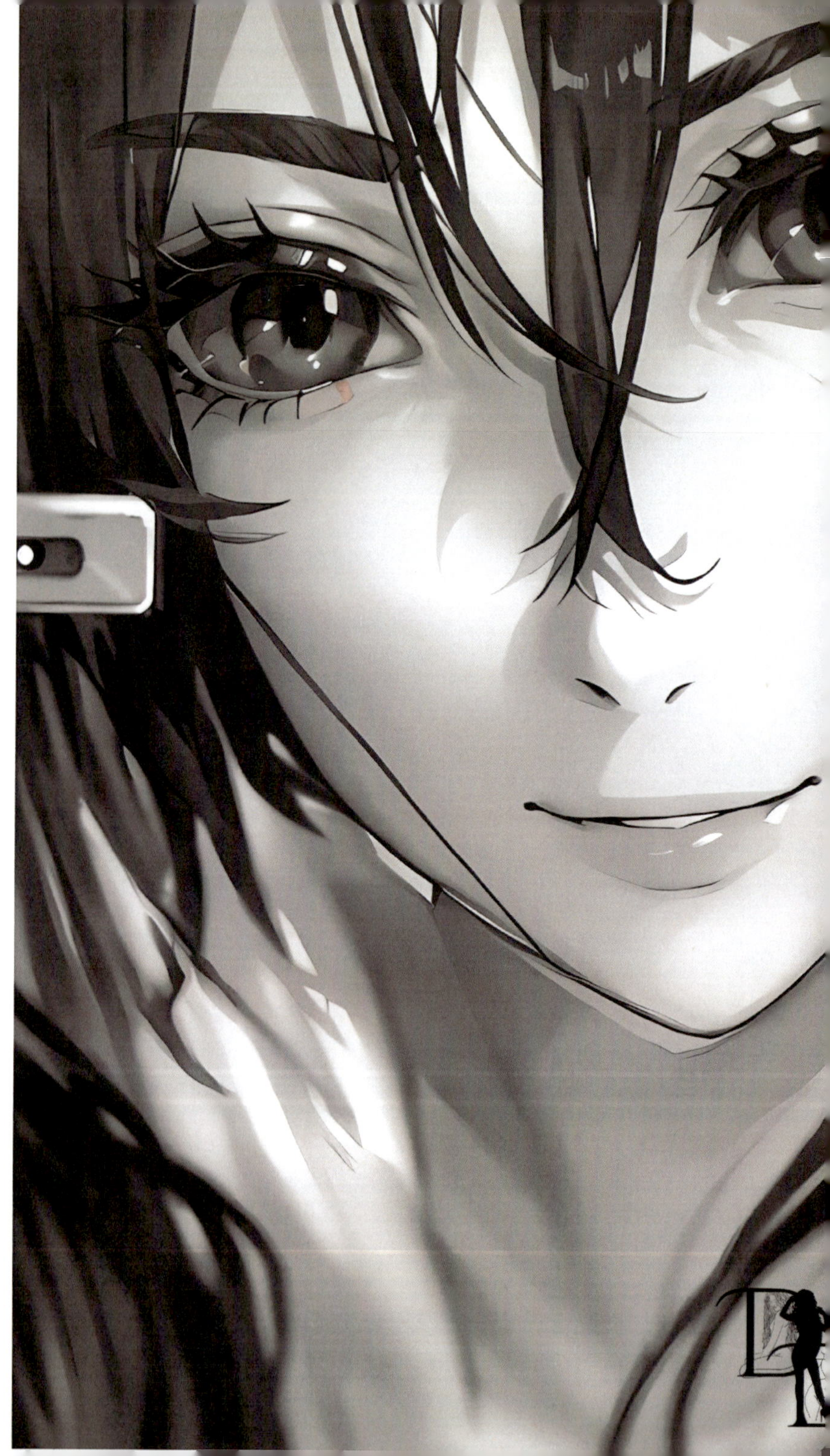

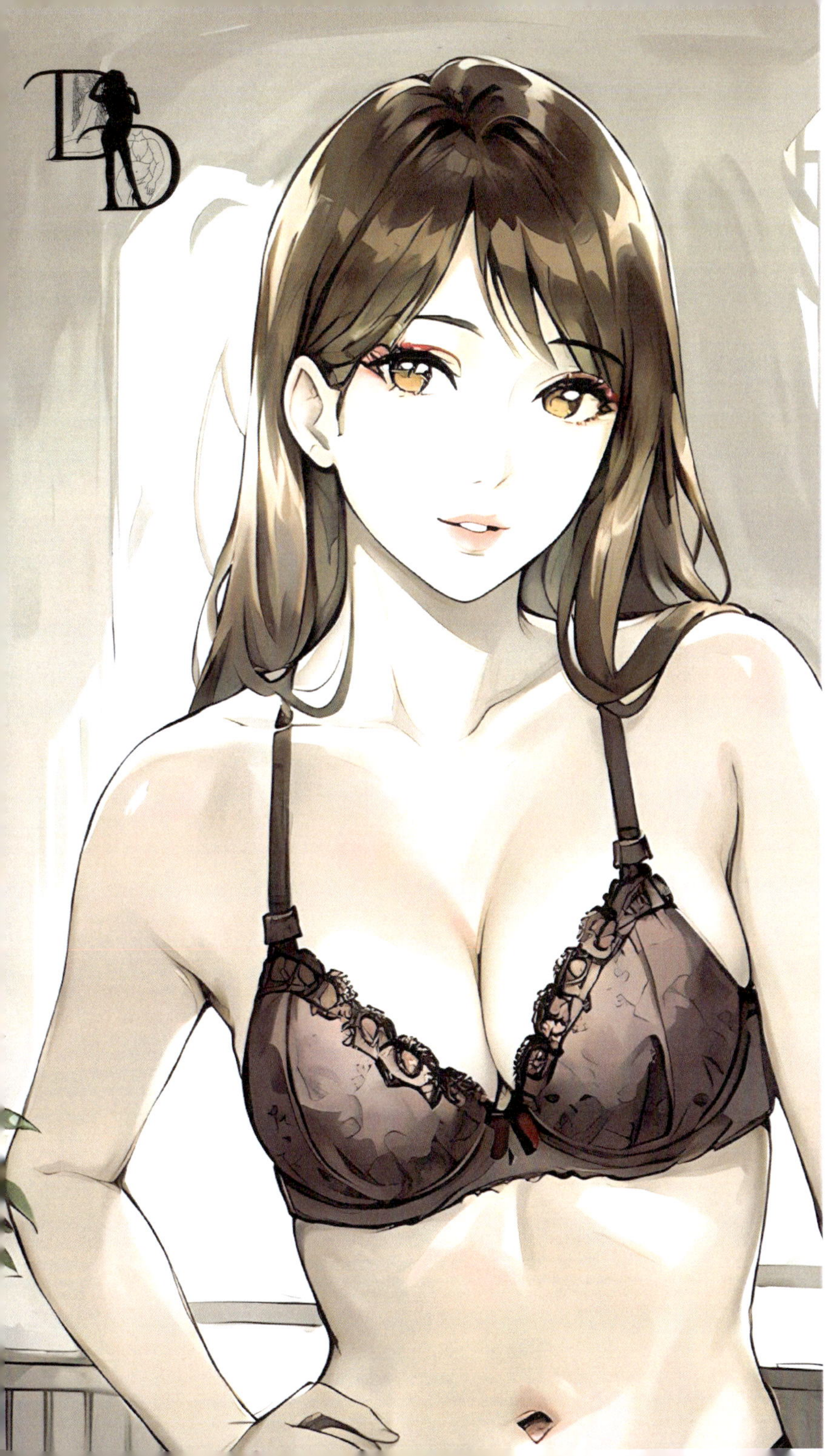

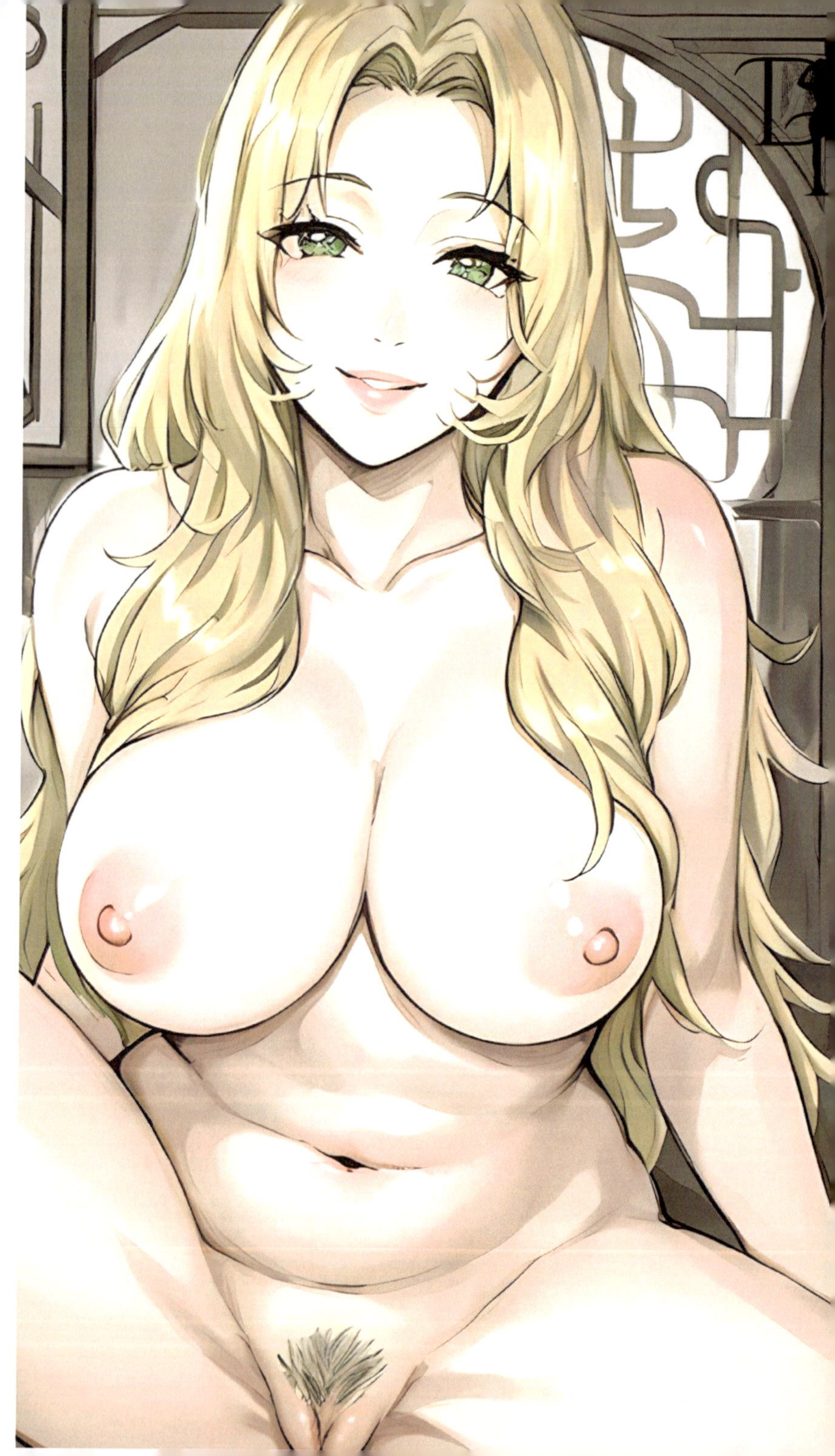

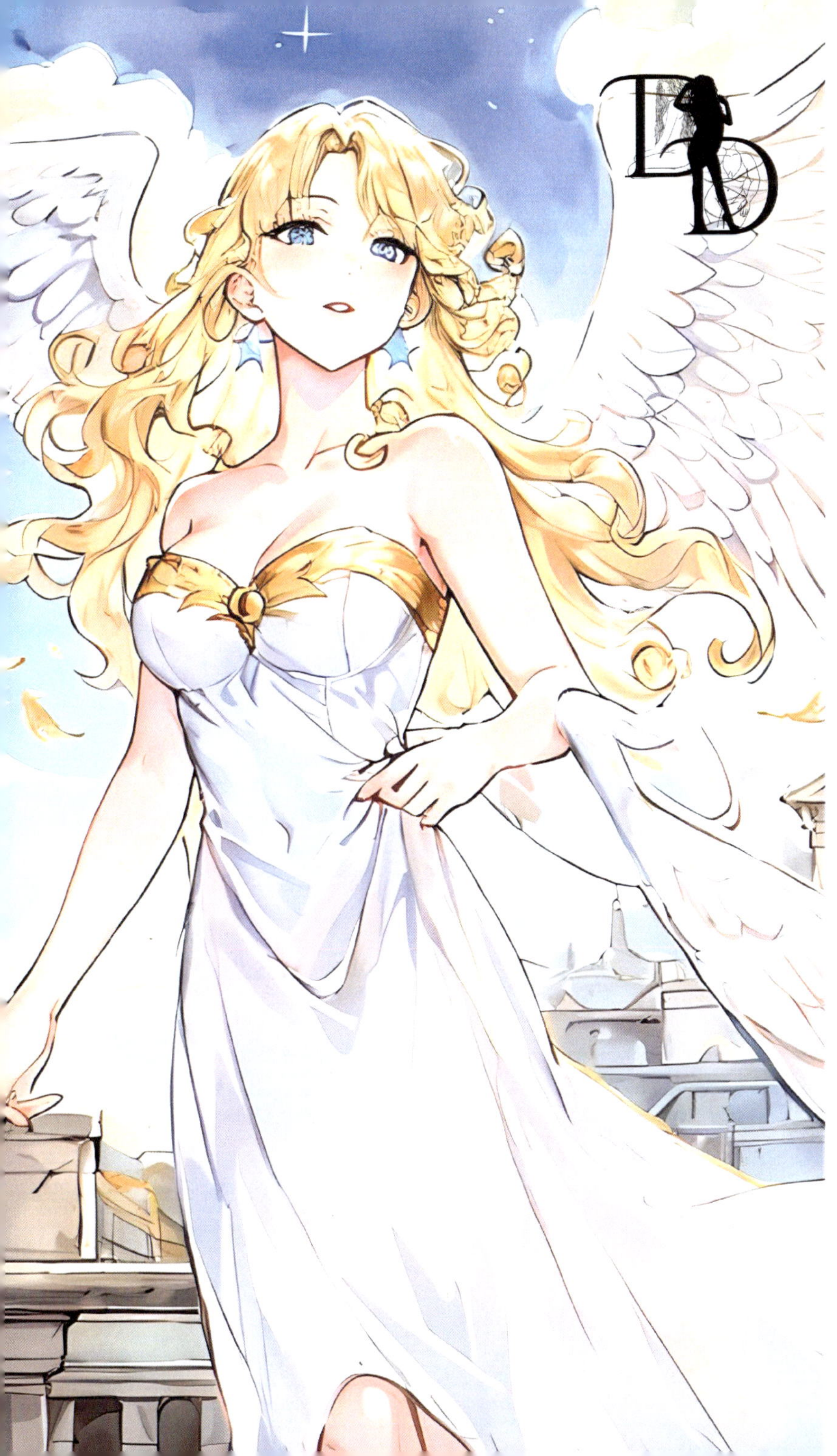

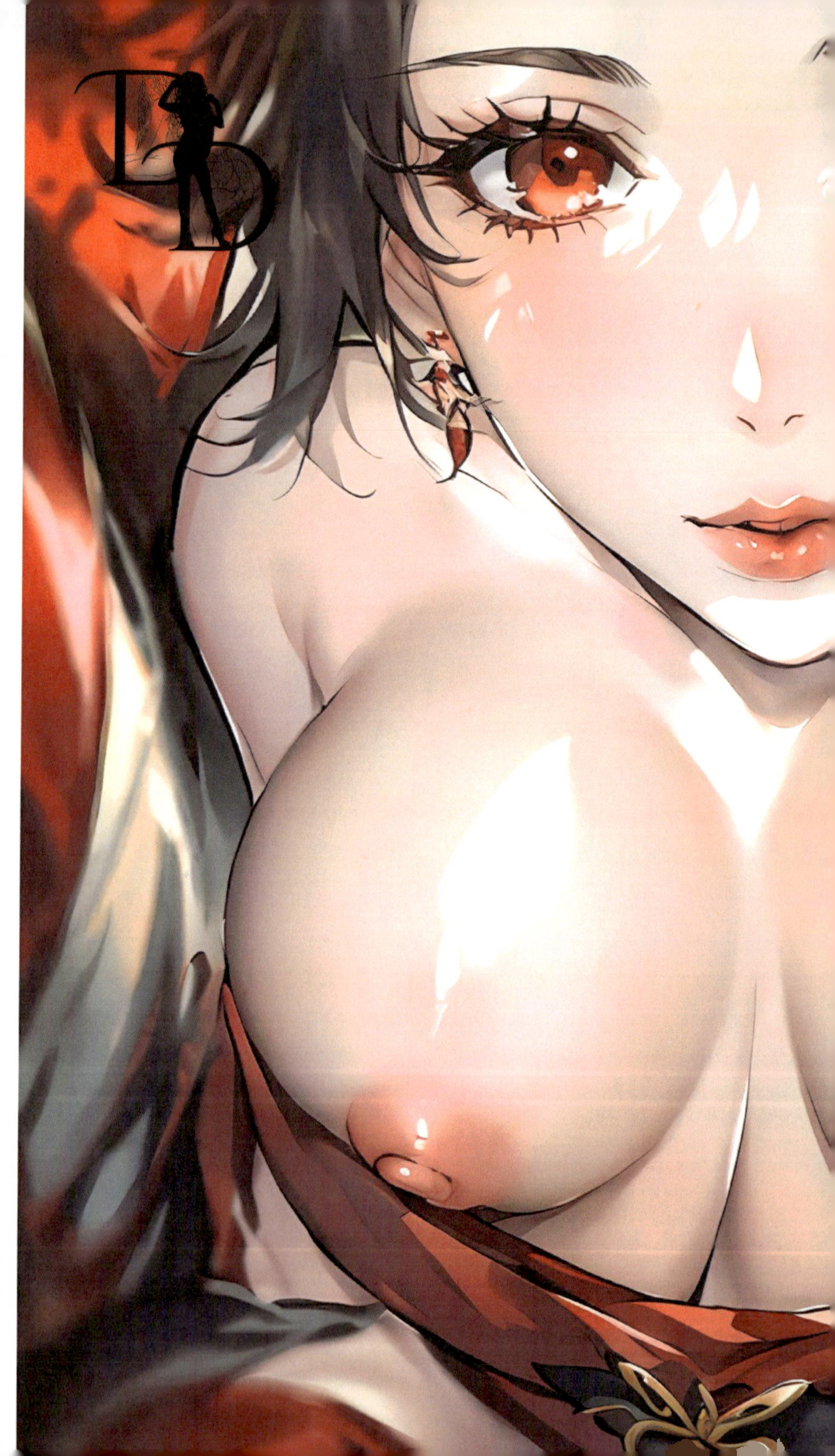

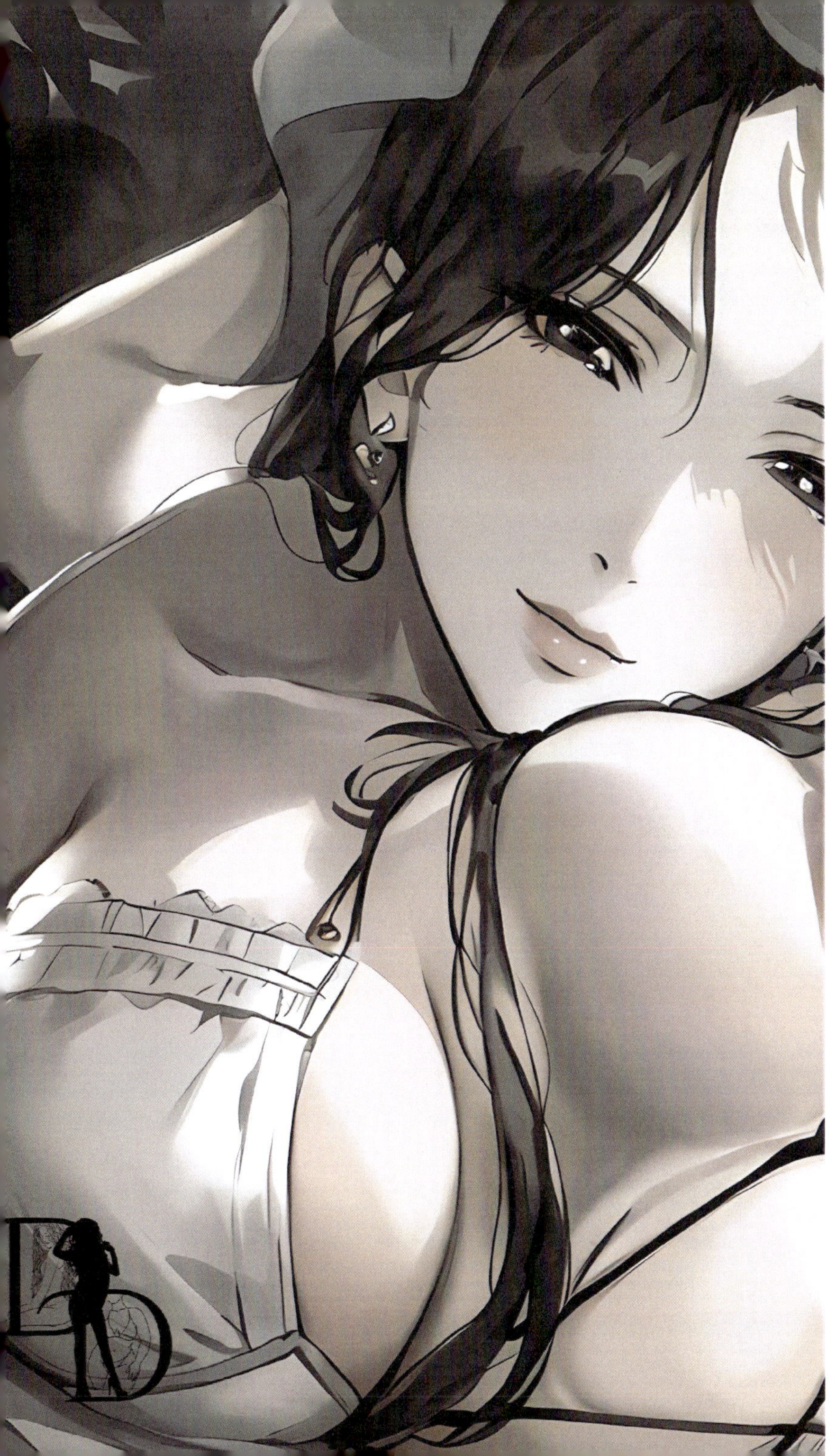

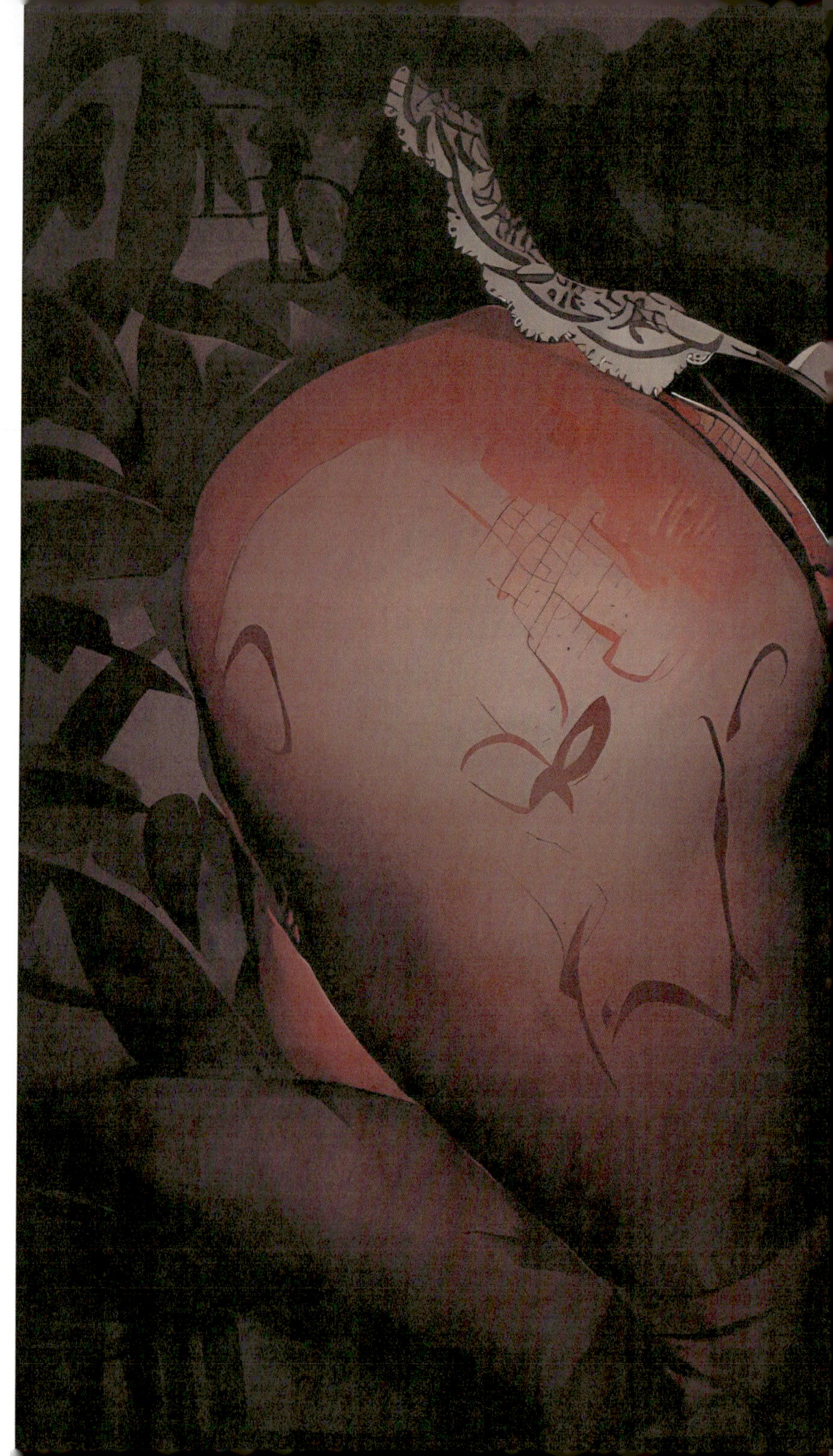

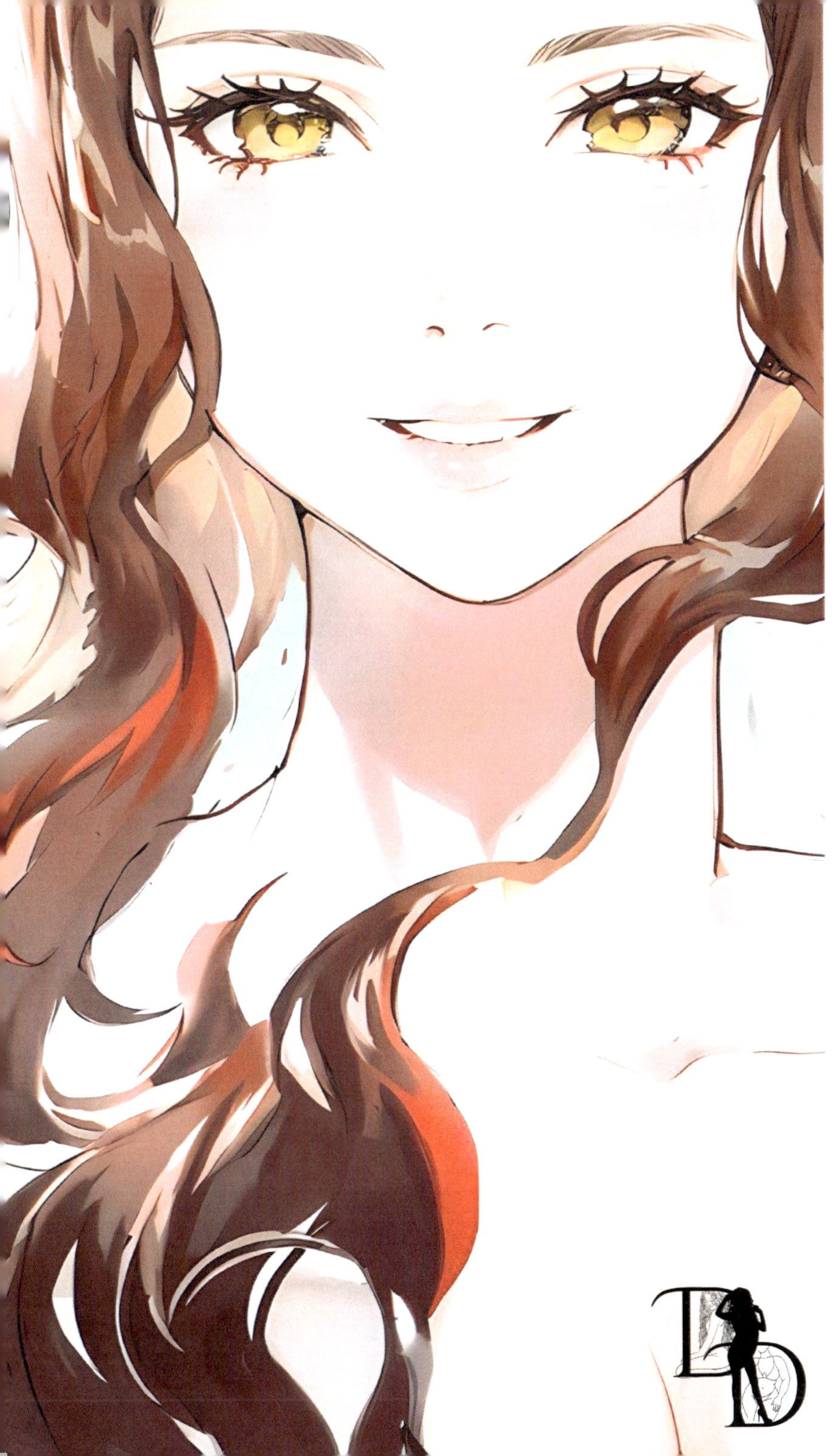

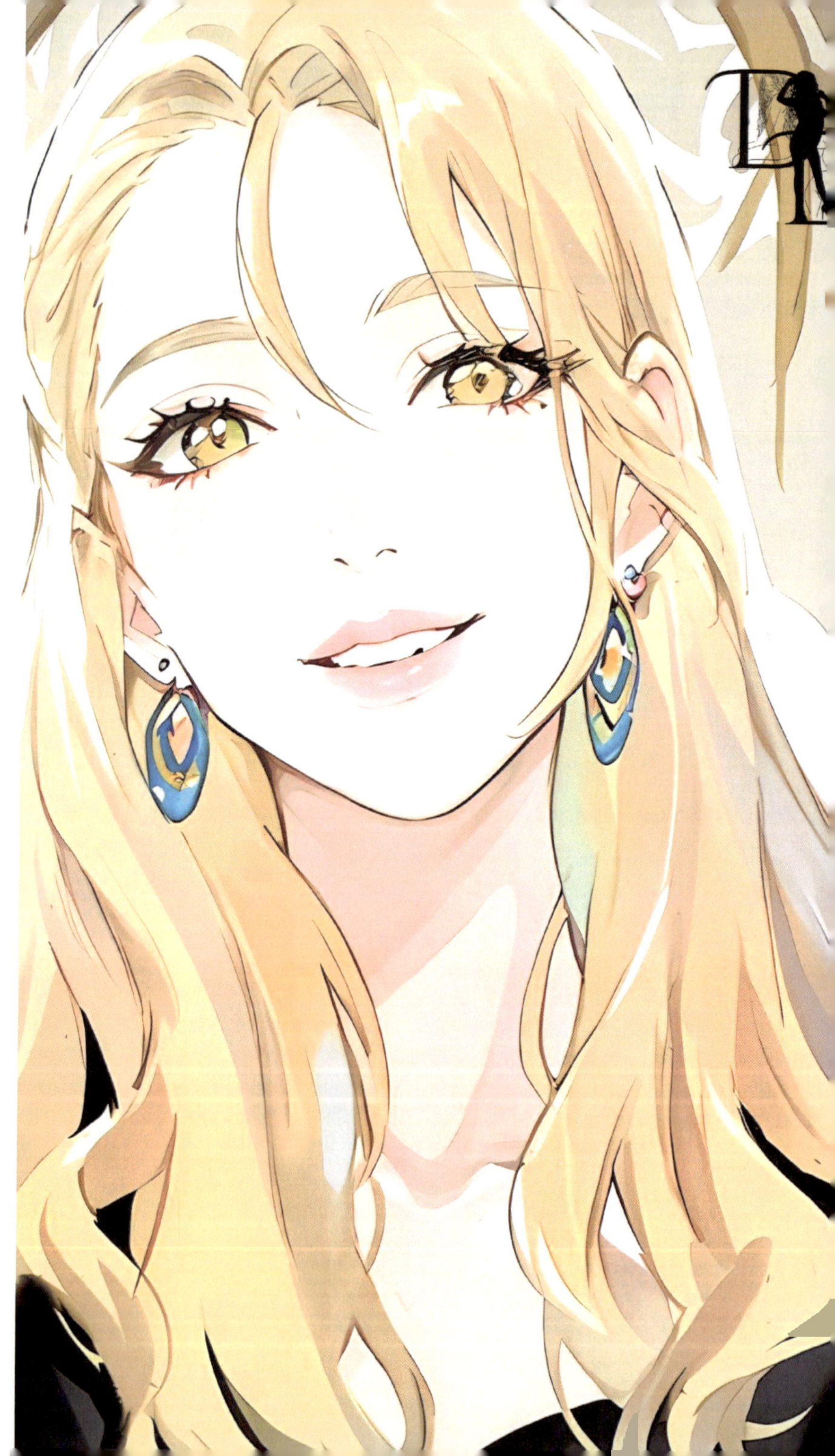

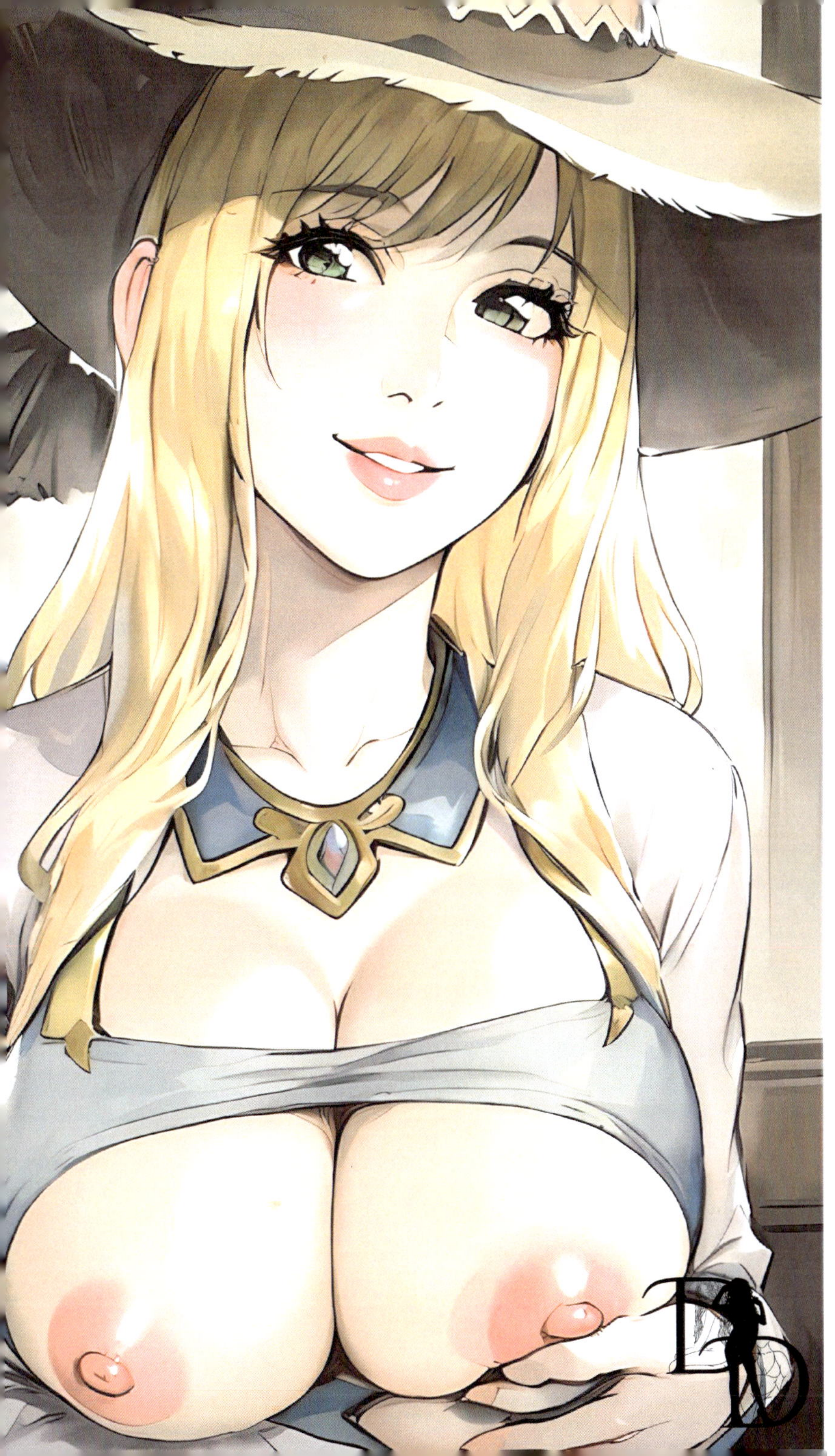

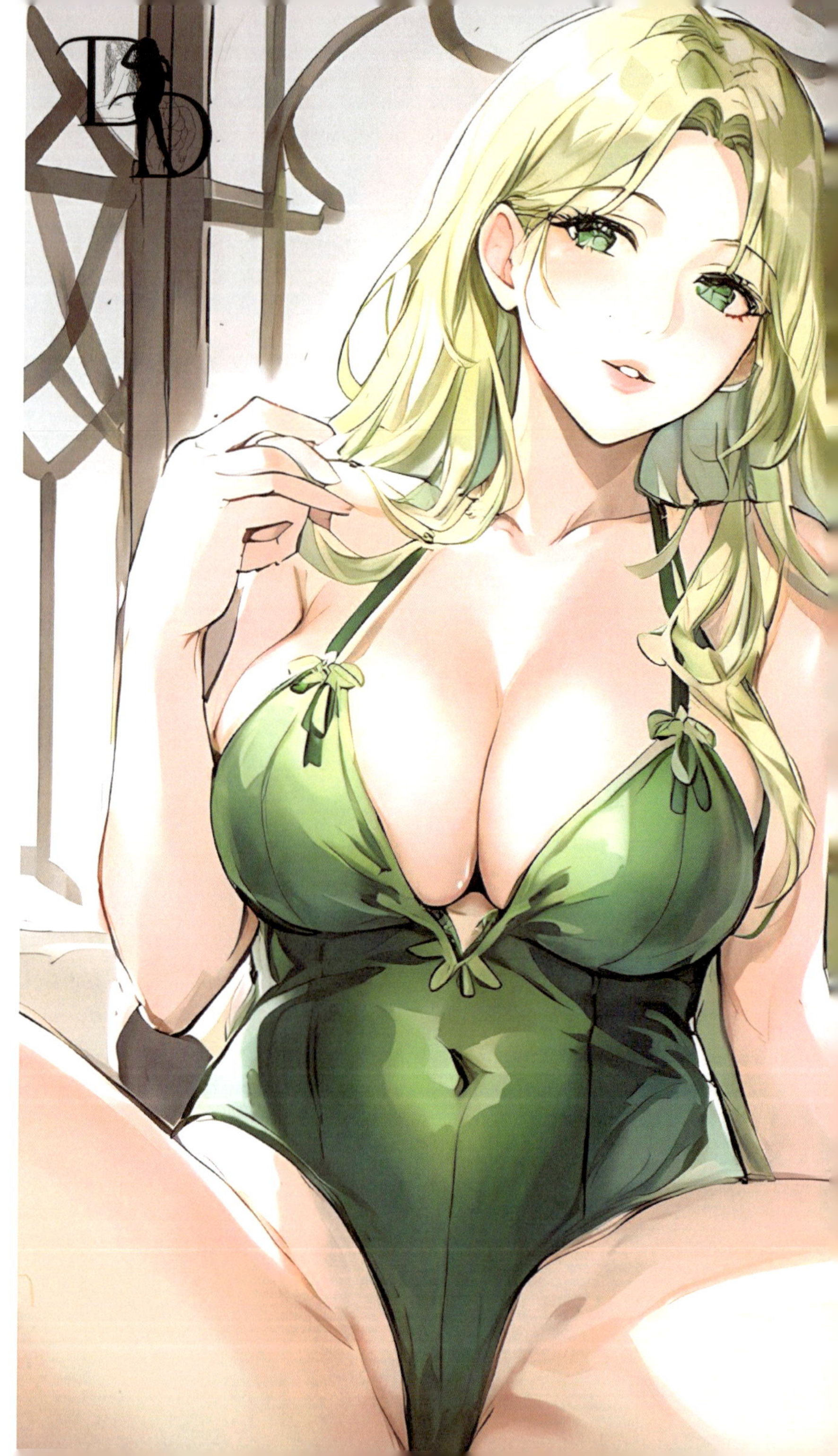

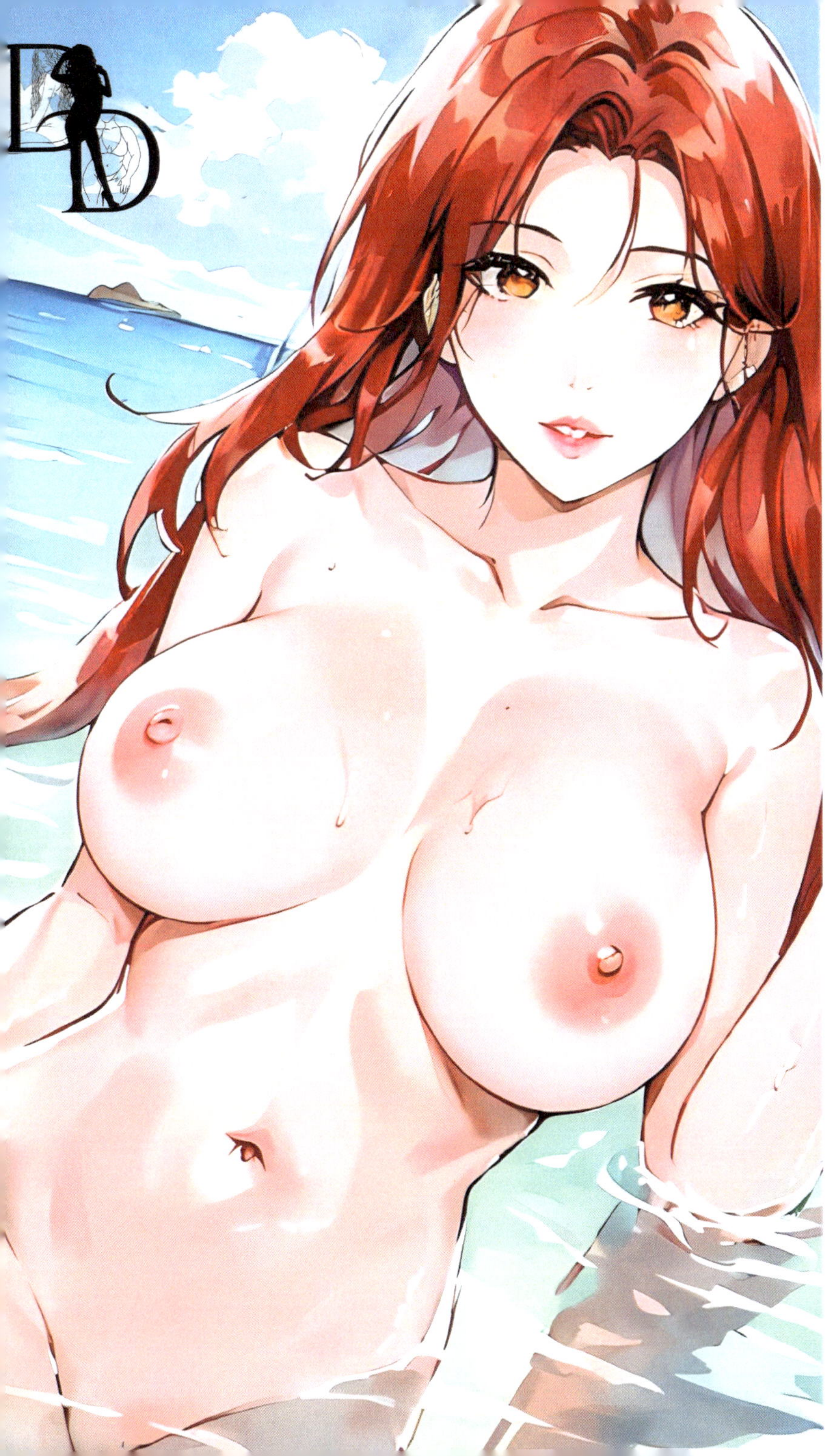

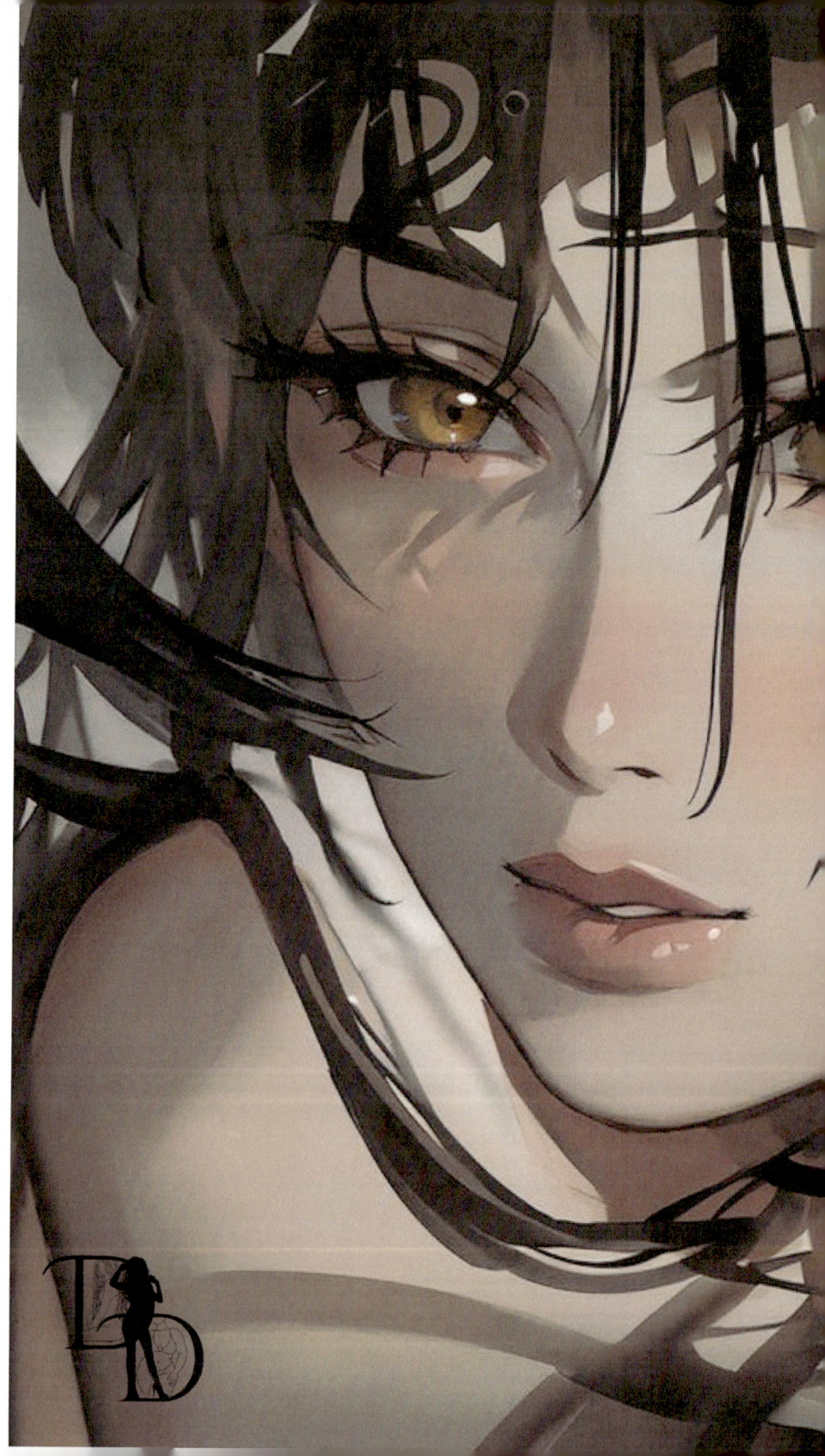

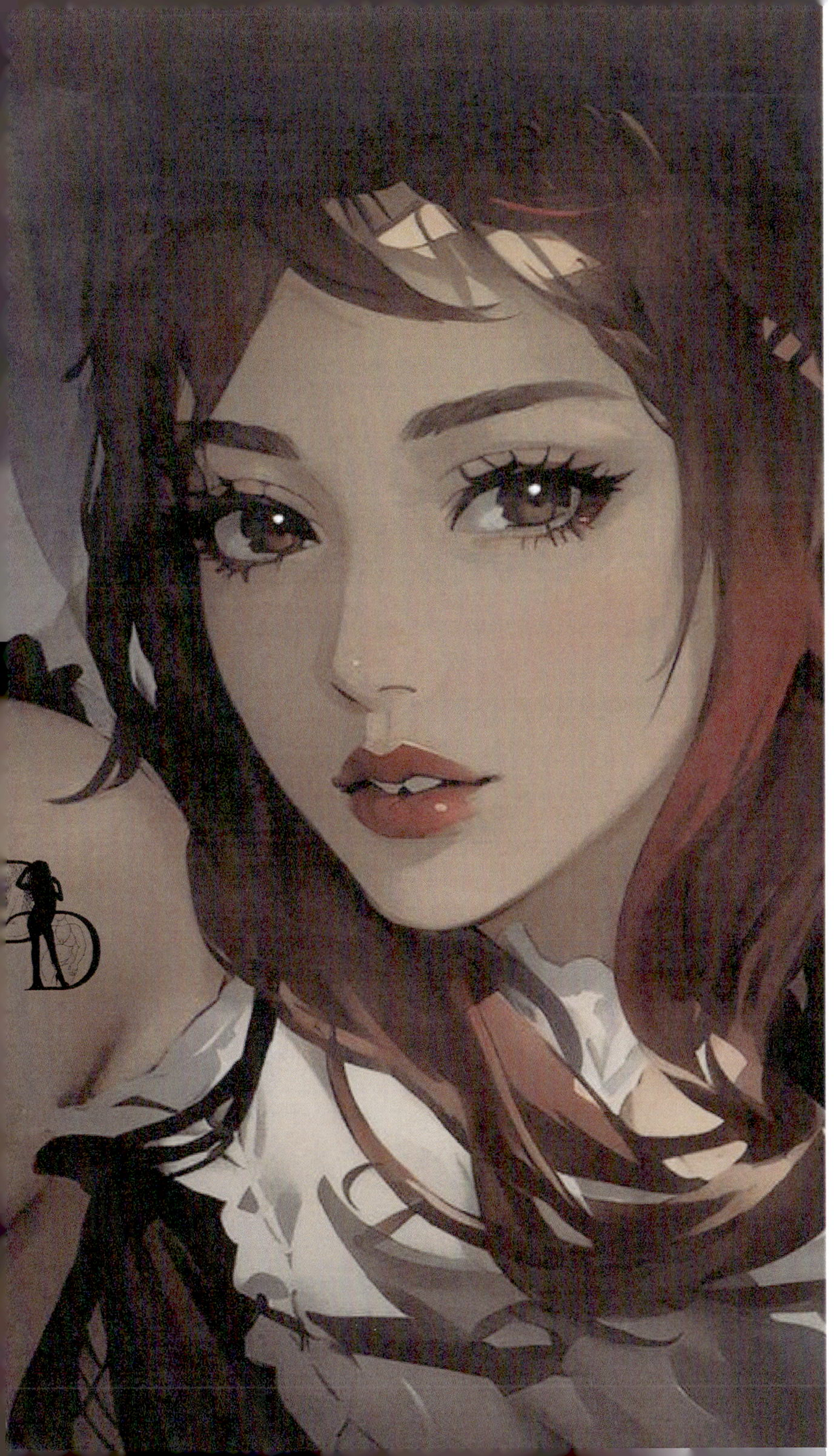

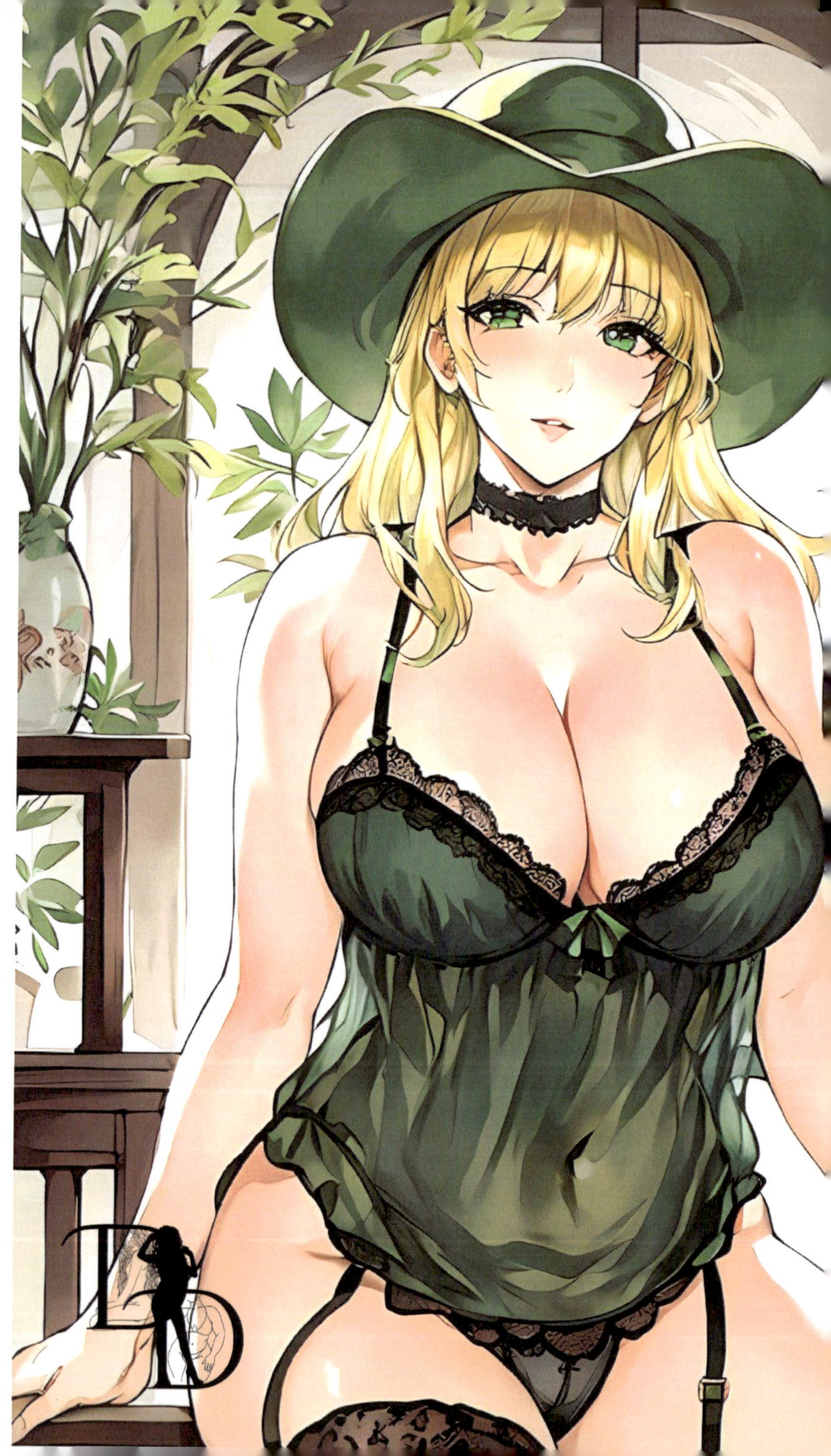

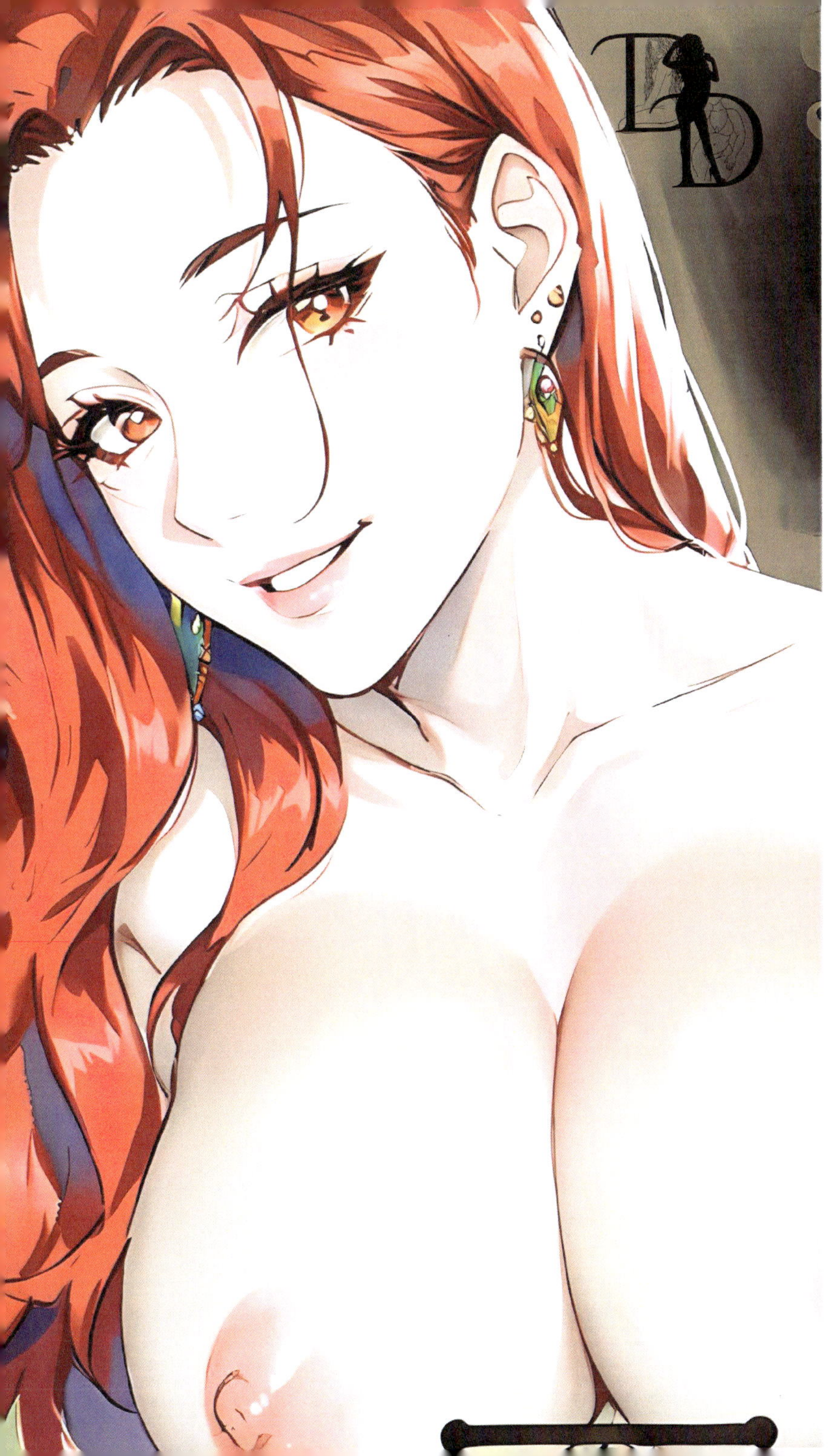

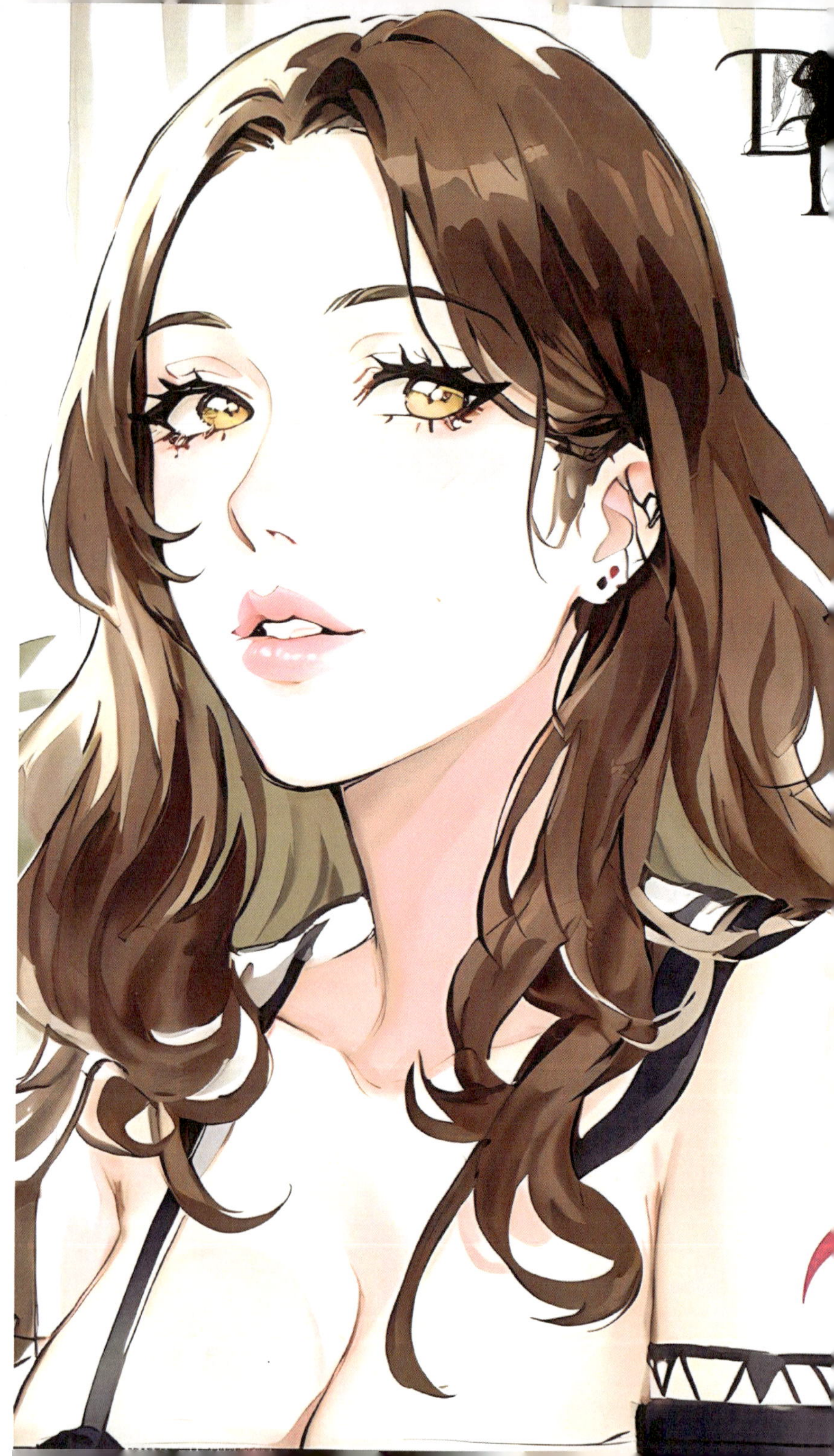

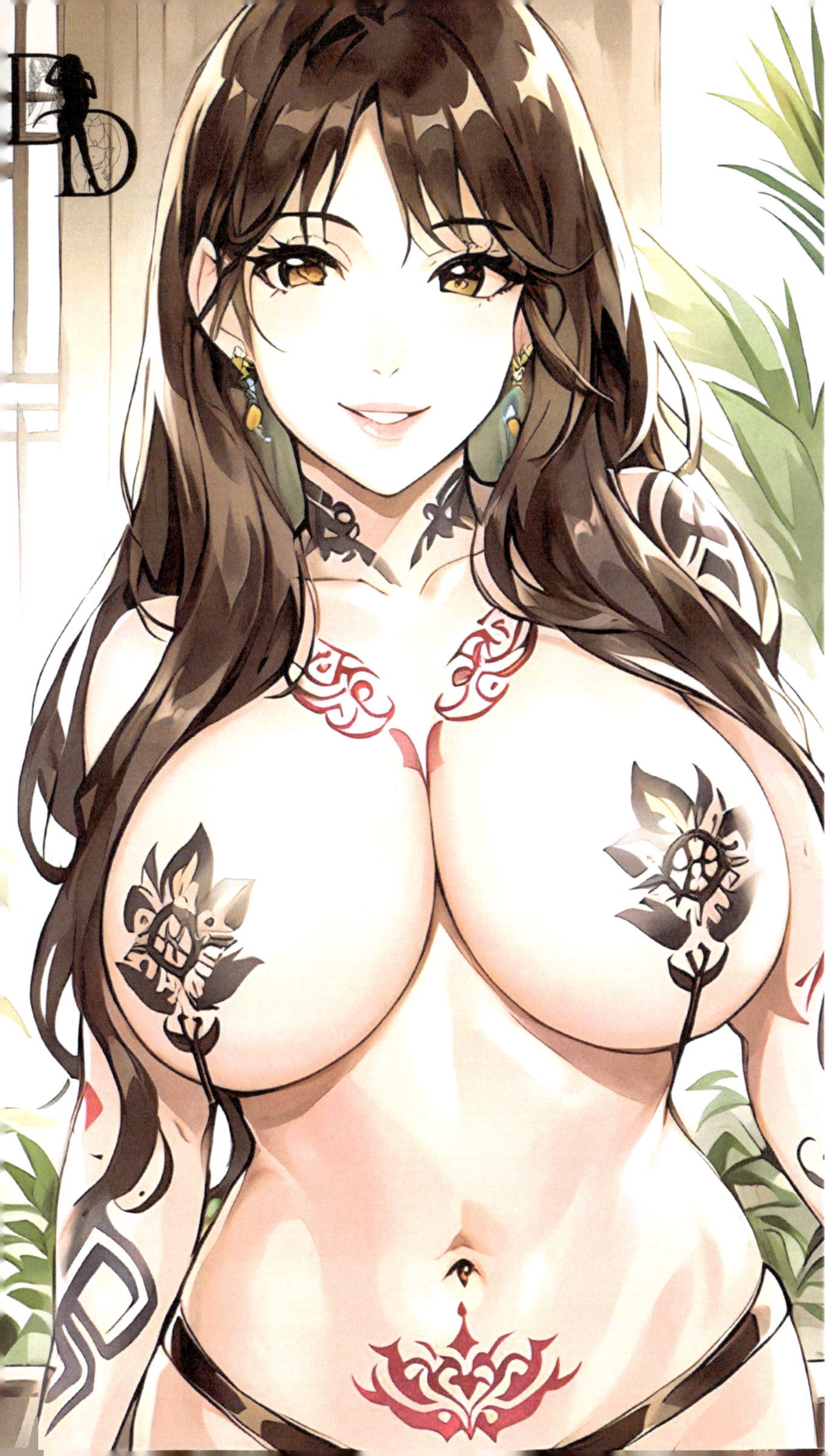

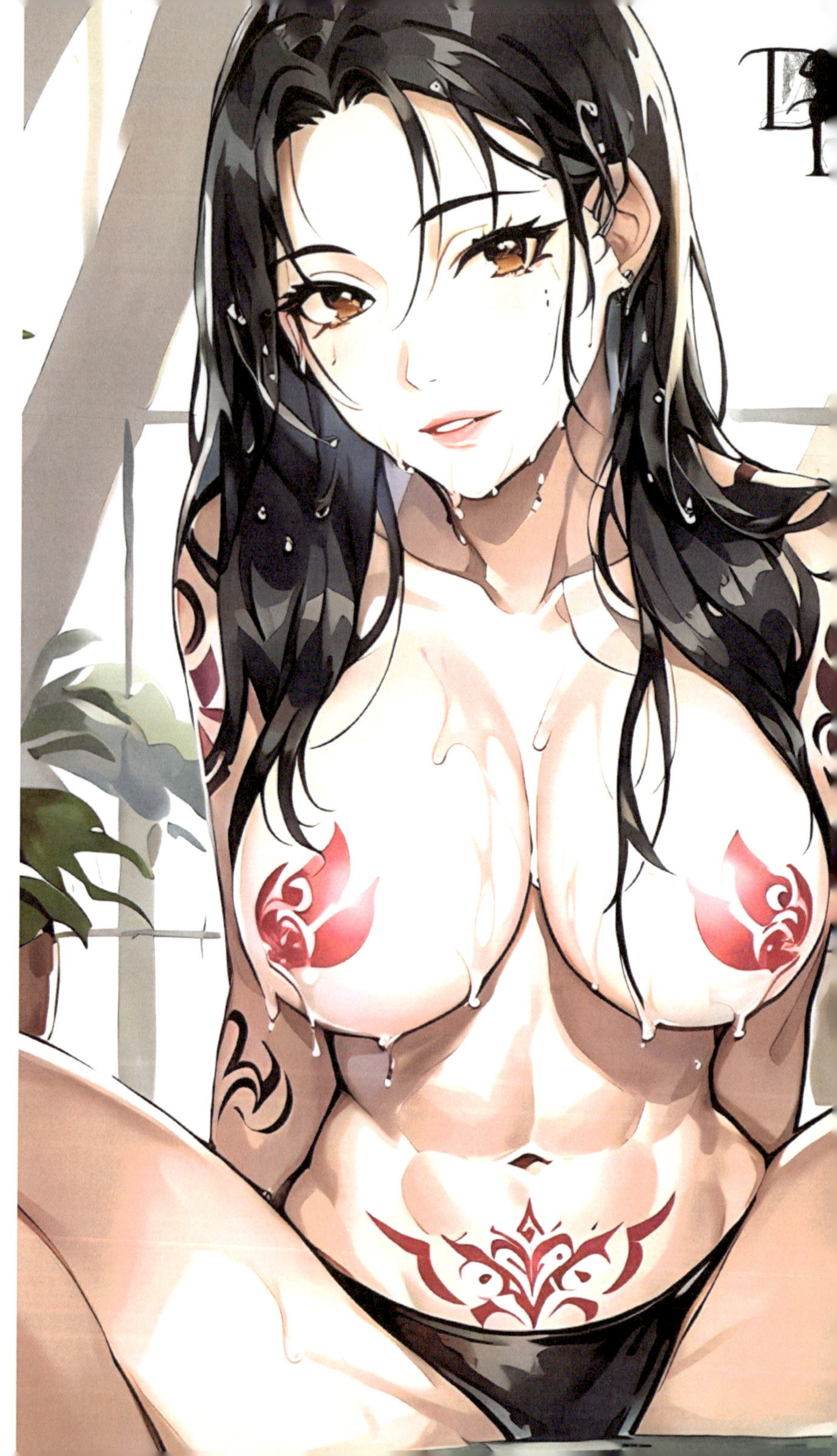

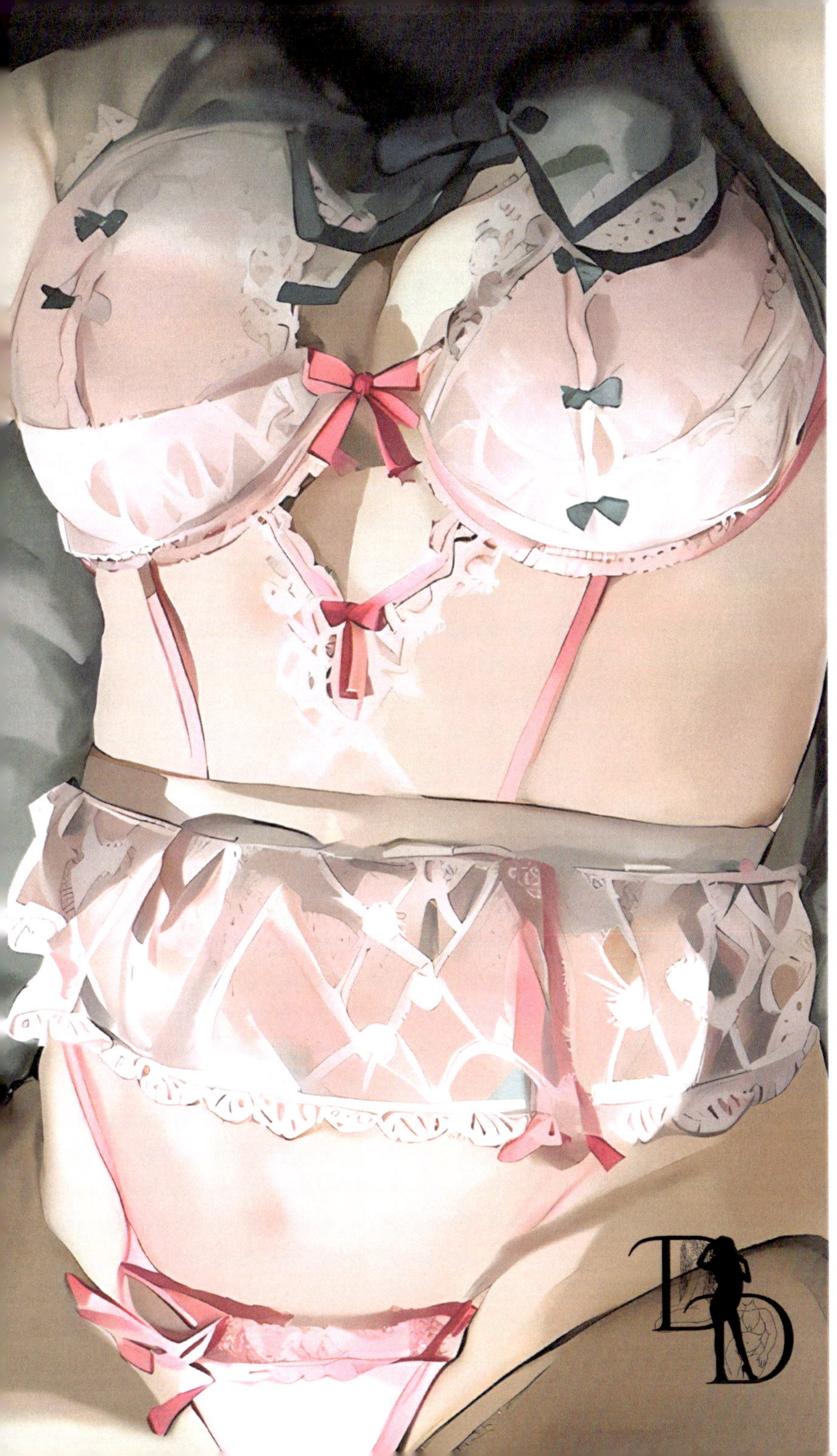

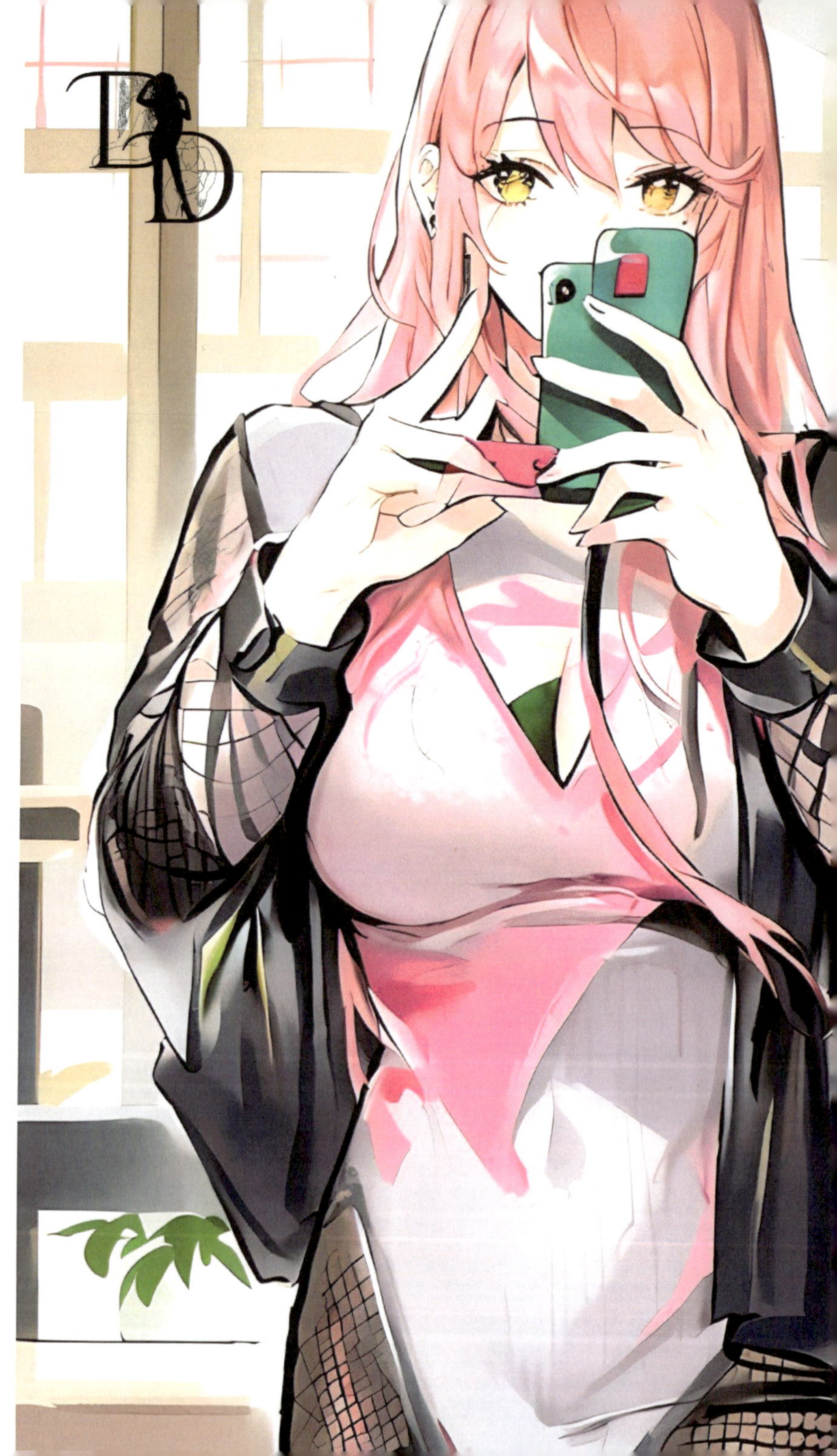